SCHENECTADY
TROLLEY HUB OF EASTERN NEW YORK

Eric H. Allen, Ph.D., P.E.

America Through Time®
Adding Color to American History

Front cover: Fonda, Johnstown & Gloversville "Bullet" car no. 128 begins a trip back to Gloversville from downtown Schenectady in the 1930s. *(From the collection of the Efner History Center at City Hall, Schenectady)*

Rear cover: Looking west on State Street in Schenectady. *(From the collection of the Efner History Center at City Hall, Schenectady)*

America Through Time is an imprint of Fonthill Media LLC
www.through-time.com
office@through-time.com

Published by Arcadia Publishing by arrangement with Fonthill Media LLC
For all general information, please contact Arcadia Publishing:
Telephone: 843-853-2070
Fax: 843-853-0044
E-mail: sales@arcadiapublishing.com
For customer service and orders:
Toll-Free 1-888-313-2665

www.arcadiapublishing.com

First published 2021

ISBN 978-1-63499-321-0

Typeset in Minion Pro 10.5pt on 14pt
Printed and bound in England

Contents

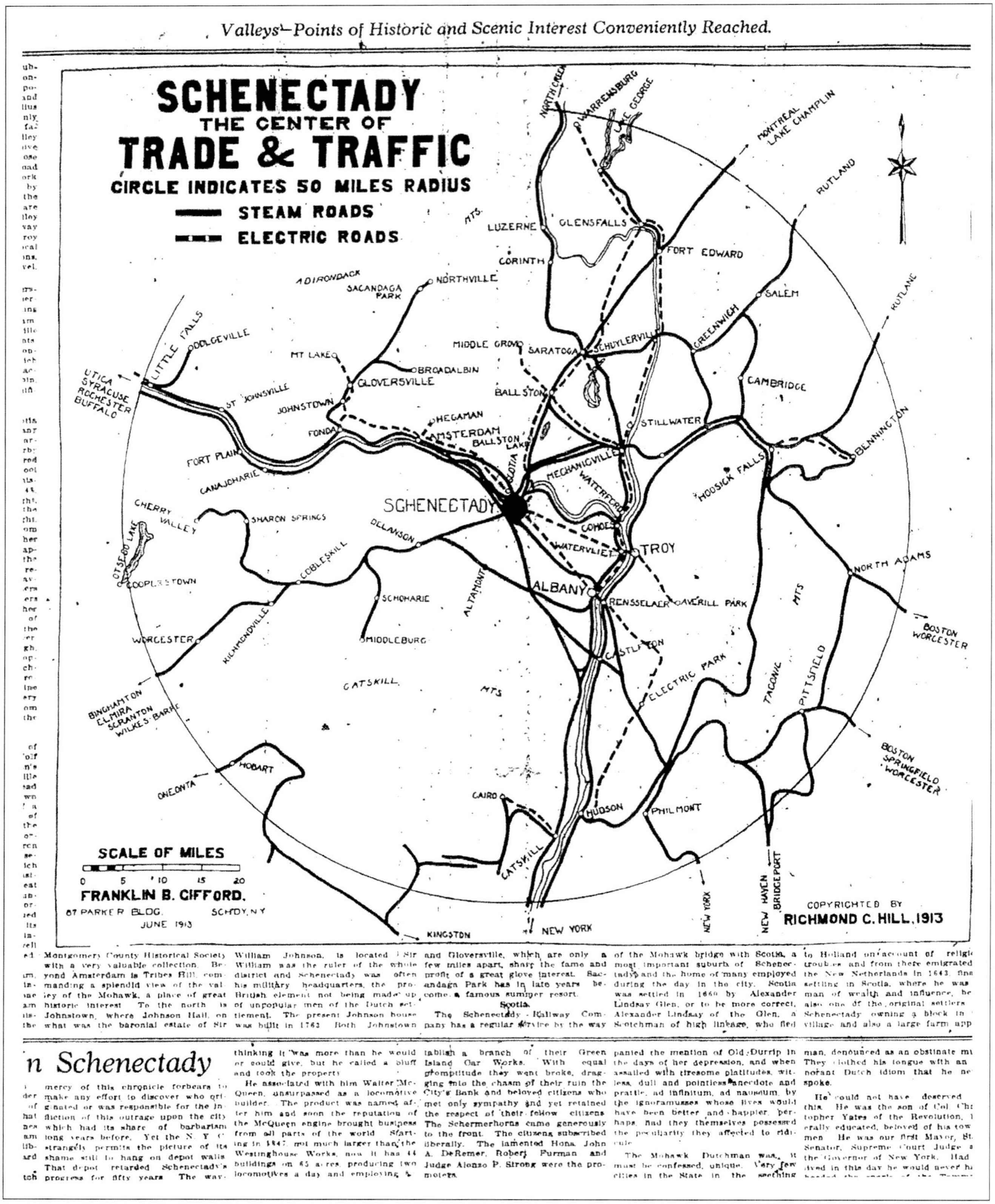

The beginning of the twentieth century was a time of enormous growth for Schenectady. General Electric and Alco, which employed many city residents, made Schenectady known as the city that "lights and hauls the world." In 1913, the *Schenectady Union-Star* published a series of articles highlighting the many qualities of the local area, which included the city's status as a transportation hub. (*Schenectady Union-Star, Schenectady County Public Library*)

Foreword

The story of electric rail transportation in Schenectady is one that mirrors the development of urban transportation throughout America in many ways, but it is also one that has its own peculiar local characteristics. Most notably, Schenectady had some of the finest amenities for street railway passengers in the nation, if not the world. Both Schenectady Railway and the Fonda, Johnstown and Gloversville Railroad constructed high-quality trackage and invested significant amounts of money above and beyond what was needed for basic service. These investments included a Beaux-Arts waiting room with 45-foot-tall ceilings, the longest trolley bridge in the world, and a distinctive fleet of vehicles ranging from interurban cars with mahogany interiors and plush seats to "Bullet" cars capable of traveling at 90 mph. All of this development took place while coping daily with some of the most concentrated rush hour traffic found anywhere.

Although books covering aspects of Schenectady's trolley history have been published previously (as shown in the bibliography), a primary focus of this book is the chronology and location of the streetcar and interurban routes partially or wholly in Schenectady. To date, the author is unaware of the publication of a more thorough, accurate, and complete treatment of these particular subtopics. It is hoped that this book can also provide the reader with a brief overview of the geographic development of the city of Schenectady. Much of this development took place in tandem with the growth of the street railway system.

Author's Note

The mileage figures given in this book are route mileage, not track mileage. Route mileages are principally estimated using a ruler and a street atlas, with many estimates corroborated by an Internet map service. Mileages are generally estimated to the nearest tenth, though in a few cases, where precise measurements are available (e.g., Public Service Commission (P.S.C.) reports), some mileages are quoted to the nearest hundredth. The exact derivation of the route and track mileage figures quoted in P.S.C. reports for the city of Schenectady is not known; the figures presented in this book indicate the author's best estimate of the elements of that calculation.

Acknowledgments

The author would like to acknowledge several organizations for their maintenance of a rich collection of historical materials; without these archives, the information in this book would likely have been impossible to find: Schenectady County Historical Society; Schenectady County Public Library; and Efner History Center at City Hall, Schenectady.

The author would like to acknowledge Fonthill Media and the company's staff for making the arrangement of this book possible, including a number of requests for fine-tuning and some last-minute additions.

The author would also like to acknowledge several individuals who made particular contributions: Mike Maloney, Librarian, Schenectady County Historical Society, who located many essential materials in the Society's Grems-Doolittle Library; Cynthia (Cindy) Seacord, Managing Archivist, Efner History Center, City of Schenectady, who located and made available many historic photographs and other materials from the Center's collection; Chris Leonard, City Historian, Efner History Center, City of Schenectady, for the same reasons; Alan Sutton, president, Fonthill Media, who personally sent acceptance and support of this project; Jamie Hardwick, project editor, Fonthill Media, for working through a number of requests and comments in the final stages of review; Kena Longabaugh, for a top-quality book cover; Robert Emerson and my brother, Scott O. Allen, who came to Schenectady for a weekend to take professional photographs for this book; my parents, Owen F. and Candace H. Allen, who shared and supported my love of transportation; my sister, Deborah L. Allen, for her love and support; and God, for all of the gifts He has given me.

1

Schenectady's Belated Horsecar Line (1887–1891)

Although Schenectady was New York's fourth incorporated city (in 1798), it was lagging behind its neighboring cities in the mid-1880s, at least in the realm of public transportation. Horsecars had been operating in Troy since 1861 and in Albany since 1863; the Mohawk valley communities of Johnstown, Gloversville, and even Fonda also had horsecar companies operating in the 1870s. Schenectady still had no streetcars operating as the year 1887 dawned, but that would soon change. The Schenectady Street Railway Company was incorporated on February 25, 1886, and received a franchise from the city on March 19, 1886, to operate animal-powered streetcars on a 1.8-mile single-track route over Washington Avenue and State Street from the Mohawk River bridge to Brandywine Avenue.

Construction was hampered by high demand for materials and harsh winter weather, requiring the company to obtain three extensions of the deadline for completing the work from the city council. The line faced legal peril as well, as a state law passed on March 22, 1886, threatened to invalidate the line's franchise. Assemblyman Edward D. Cutler managed to obtain a modification of the law at the last hour of the 1885–86 legislative session. The line's completion was celebrated with a silver spike ceremony on July 15, 1887, and the railway opened for service the next day.

The street railway company had "5 horsecars, 4 sleighs, and 30 horses." The barn and stable for the cars and horses were located at the Brandywine Avenue end. The franchise required a minimum of hourly service between the hours of 6.30 a.m. and 9 p.m. while allowing a maximum fare of 5 cents for a single trip regardless of distance traveled. Though the franchise permitted a narrow-gauge railway (3 feet 6 inches), the railway was built to standard gauge (4 feet 8½ inches).

The horsecar railway ran along the edge of the Stockade—the historic, primarily residential district located at the site of the initial settlement of the city in 1661. From there, the line ran through the commercial center of the city, which was developing along State Street just east of the Erie Canal and the two railroads (the New York Central and the Delaware and Hudson (D&H)). The horsecar line then continued for about a mile out the route of the Albany and Schenectady Turnpike, which was built on an arrow-straight path between Albany and Schenectady and opened in 1805.

The street railway's formation happened to coincide with another event that would greatly influence and define Schenectady: the decision of Thomas Alva Edison to move the Edison General Works company to the city in 1886. The operations of General Electric (G.E.), Schenectady Locomotive Works (which became part of Alco in 1901), and the city's street railway would be intertwined for decades.

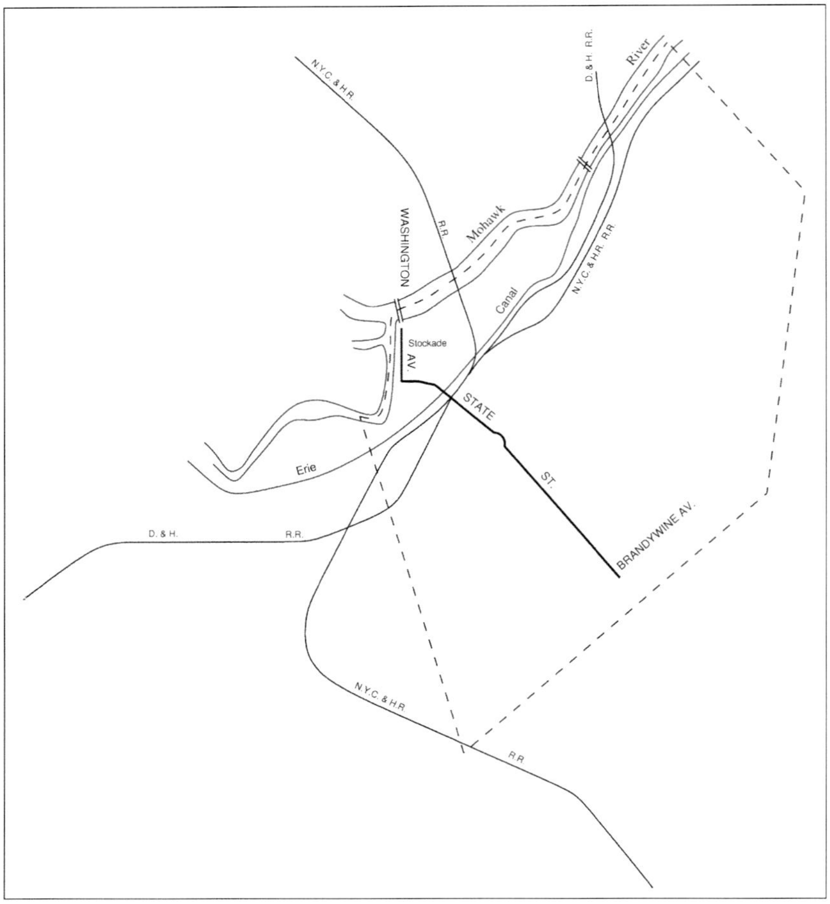

Left: Route of Schenectady Street Railway, 1887 (length: 1.8 miles). (*Map by author*)

Below: Horsecar no. 1 on State St. crossing the railroad tracks. (*From the collection of the Efner History Center at City Hall, Schenectady*)

2

Electrification and Extension
(1891–1893)

The Schenectady Street Railway started operation just as electricity was about to revolutionize urban transportation. Frank Sprague would lead the conversion to electric streetcars in Richmond, VA, the very next year (1888), and the technology spread rapidly throughout the U.S. in just a few years. However, at the time, electric traction was still unproven, and many streetcar companies were turning to a more mature technology: cable. In cities like Baltimore and Cleveland, the various horsecar companies grappled with the decision of which technology was the better investment. Many chose cable.

In Schenectady, cables do not seem to have been seriously considered for motive power. The railway's petition for a franchise modification to permit a new propulsion method only mentioned electricity and its virtues. The city council approved this modification in 1890, and the Schenectady Street Railway Company accordingly completed the conversion to electric power in 1891. Six new electric-powered streetcars were built by Gilbert Car Works, which was leasing shop space in Schenectady at the time. The first run of an electric streetcar in Schenectady took place on the evening of July 2. Though lacking the formality of the ceremony that marked the opening of the line, the inaugural electric run, made by car no. 6, carried its share of dignitaries and was celebrated by a crowd of hundreds. Electric streetcars began revenue service on July 3, 1891, and the company auctioned off its horses shortly afterward. The old horsecars were retained and converted to electric use by adding apparatus for electric propulsion; they were principally used during times of lighter patronage.

At the same time, the company sought to expand its trackage. The first extension opened for service on July 26, 1891, when streetcars began running southeast on State Street beyond Brandywine Avenue to Elm Street across the city line (which was then located at Division Street). Although the railway company had petitioned the city council for approval of this extension on July 15, approval was not officially granted until August 11.[1] The terminus of this 0.4-mile extension would be located two blocks further, at Locust Street (now Elder Street), for many years. Brandywine Park, with an entrance at Elm and Albany Streets, was a significant source of traffic for this extension. The newly created park was the site of many concerts, picnics, and other such events.

In December 1890, the city council had approved an extension of the street railway service in a southwesterly direction to the Bellevue area in the town of Rotterdam. Starting from State and Church Streets, the new route followed Church and Fuller Streets and then proceeded on Rotterdam Street to the city line and beyond. In Rotterdam, the streetcar tracks followed Broadway and Campbell Avenue to 17th Street. This 2.3-mile extension opened on October 17, 1891. This extension connected the growing works of the newly renamed Edison General Electric Company and a new residential development on the hillside overlooking these works to the center of the city.[2] Bellevue thus became one of the earliest "trolley suburbs" in the nation. Another park (Bellevue Park) was also located at this end of the line.

The company added open cars in 1893. Six open cars built by Jones Car Company were purchased, with the first two (nos. 13 and 14) entering service on June 11. Such cars were part of the fleet of most trolley companies of the era. These cars were tremendously popular with passengers, particularly in an era without air conditioning.

Schenectady Railway car no. 6, the first electric car to operate in Schenectady, is shown in 1902. (*From the collection of the Schenectady County Historical Society*)

Schenectady Railway car no. 6, the first electric car to operate in Schenectady. (*From the collection of the Efner History Center at City Hall, Schenectady*)

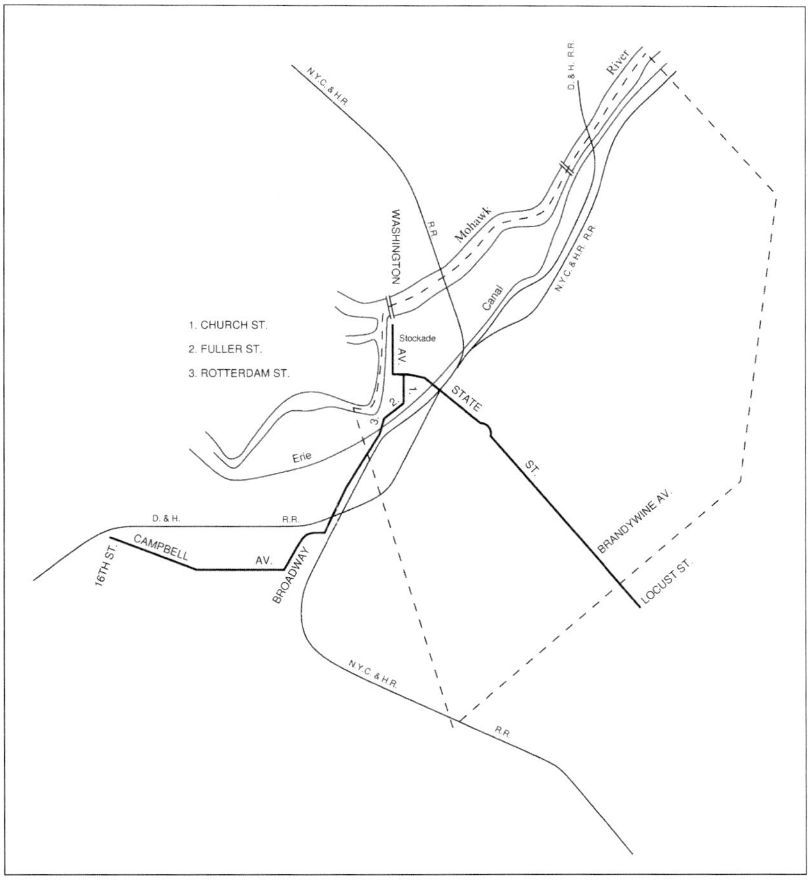

Right: Routes of Schenectady Street Railway, 1893 (total length: 4.5 miles). (*Map by author*)

Below: Open car on Washington Avenue. (*From the collection of the Efner History Center at City Hall, Schenectady*)

3

G.E. Takes Over

(1893–1899)

Although the Schenectady Street Railway Company made relatively distant areas much more accessible to Schenectady's commercial and industrial districts, the company was not financially successful and entered receivership in 1893. The national economic conditions at the time certainly did not help; the Panic of 1893 was beginning. Plans to construct a new branch on Nott Terrace and Union Street were abandoned.[1] In October 1893, with the approval of the city council, the company suspended service between the corner of State and Church Streets and the Mohawk River bridge, citing low demand for service. This suspension was made permanent in October 1894. The 0.3-mile branch was abandoned, and the tracks were pulled up.

The assets of the bankrupt company were sold at foreclosure for $100,000 (the minimum price allowed by the court) at public auction on January 3, 1895. The purchasers soon organized a new company, the Schenectady Railway Company, on February 11, 1895. Aided by an improving national economy, the fortunes of the railway turned around significantly.

Schenectady Railway bought Brandywine Park in 1896. The park had begun to acquire a seedy reputation, and Schenectady Railway had a direct interest in changing this perception. The railway company performed extensive renovations and added a new dance pavilion, croquet lawns, and a picnic grove. A grand reopening took place on Saturday, May 30, 1896. Many civic groups and labor unions held group outings at the park over the years.

A relocation of the Bellevue line from Rotterdam Street to a private right-of-way within the General Electric Company's Schenectady Works was authorized in 1896. By 1898, traffic on the Bellevue line was described as "heavy." Another relocation of the line was authorized in 1899, placing it on River Road and Mill Lane to reach the crossing of the Delaware and Hudson (D&H) Railroad. From there, it resumed its original route on Broadway and Campbell Avenue. This relocation added 0.3 miles to the route.

General Electric bought the Schenectady Railway Company and the Schenectady Illuminating Company for $750,000 in 1898. Besides having an interest in transporting its own workers, G.E. recognized that the companies would be viewed as a showcase of modern electrical technology. The city's residents would be among the first in the world to enjoy the benefits of these technological developments. Schenectady had truly become "the Electric City."

One of the first improvements G.E. made to the street railway was the construction of a new car house and repair shop on Fuller Street. Located near the center of the railway system, the new facility was substantially larger and built of brick. It opened just before the end of 1899.

Under G.E. ownership, the company began to expand its routes again. Additional trackage was approved by the city council in 1899 to aid railway operations. The company was authorized to build a 0.1-mile track around the southern side of Crescent Park (now Veterans Park), completing a loop around the park. Some 0.3 miles of trackage on State Street, Washington Avenue, and Rotterdam Street was also authorized for essentially extending double track from State Street to the new Fuller Street barn.

Needing to raise money, Union College made a 75-acre tract of land just east of the campus available for sale. General Electric bought the land for $57,000 in 1899 and, through a subsidiary (the Schenectady Realty Company), developed the land as an area of high-end residential homes. The property deeds contained a number of restrictions to enhance the character of the neighborhood, including minimum lot sizes (70 × 140 feet), minimum setbacks of all buildings from the street (25 feet), and a minimum house cost ($4,000 at the time). The development became known as "the G.E. Realty Plot."

G.E. wasted no time in providing access to the new homes via its street railway subsidiary. The city council authorized a new street railway branch 1.3 miles in length on Nott Terrace, Union Street, and Union Avenue from State Street to the junction of Nott Street and Union Avenue (now Wendell Avenue) in 1899. The branch opened partway (as far as University Place) on September 30 of that year and the rest of the way to Nott Street on October 20. The initial service frequency on the branch was fifteen minutes; with the State Street branch east of Nott Terrace also having fifteen-minute service, one could expect a trolley every seven and a half minutes through the center of the city between Nott Terrace and the General Electric works.

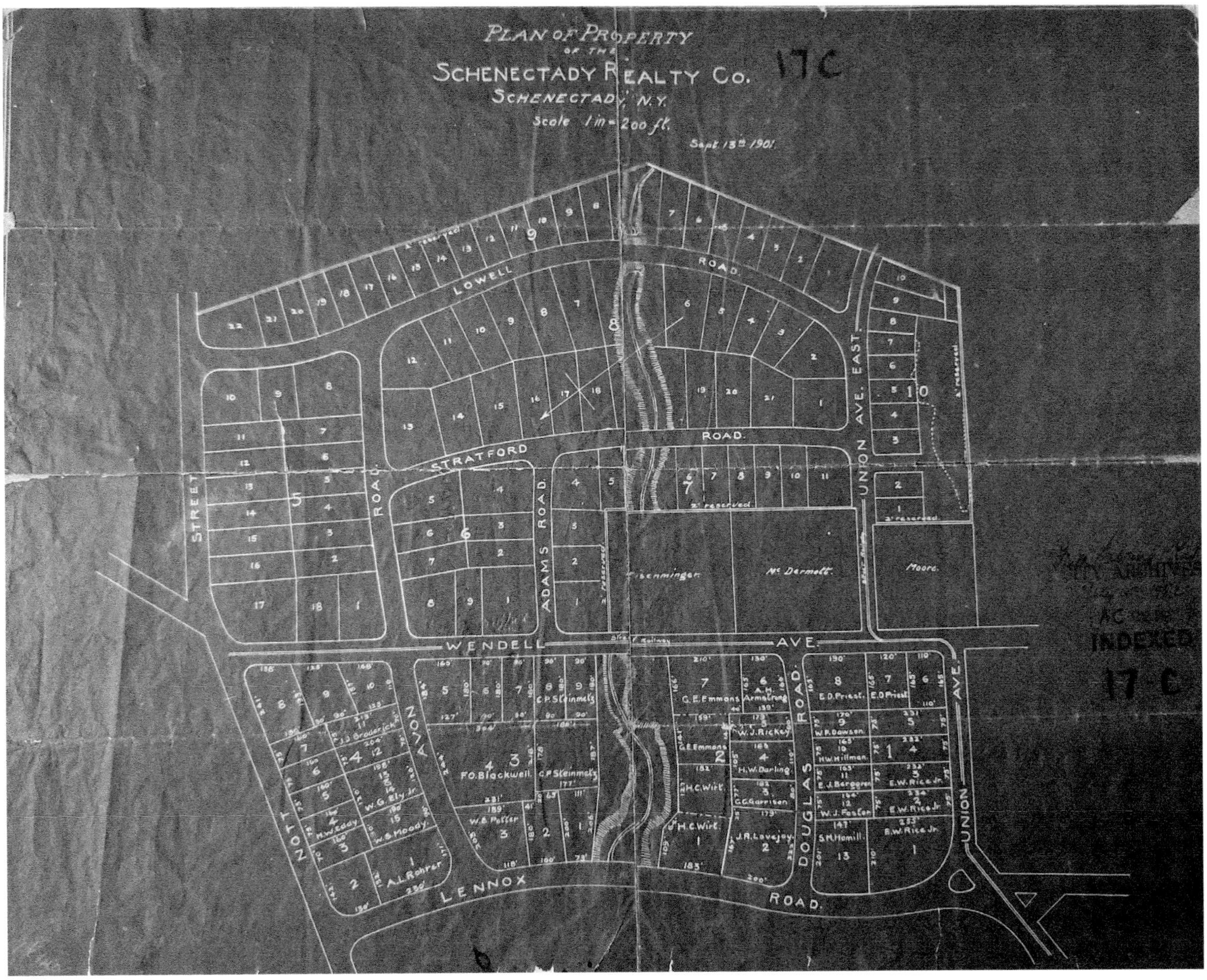

Plan of G.E. Realty Plot, 1901, showing the inclusion of the street railway in the plot. (*From the collection of the Efner History Center at City Hall, Schenectady*)

The General Electric works was established as a terminus for some trolley trips at about this time. Nearly all inbound cars from Union Avenue in particular would terminate at G.E. A loop for turning, loading, and unloading trolleys was constructed at the main gate. This location was initially designated as "G.E. Works" on trolleys but would later be known as "G.E. Loop." The loop would henceforth be a major source of passenger traffic for Schenectady Railway Company.

A 2018 view of the G.E. Realty Plot. (*Photography by Robert Emerson*)

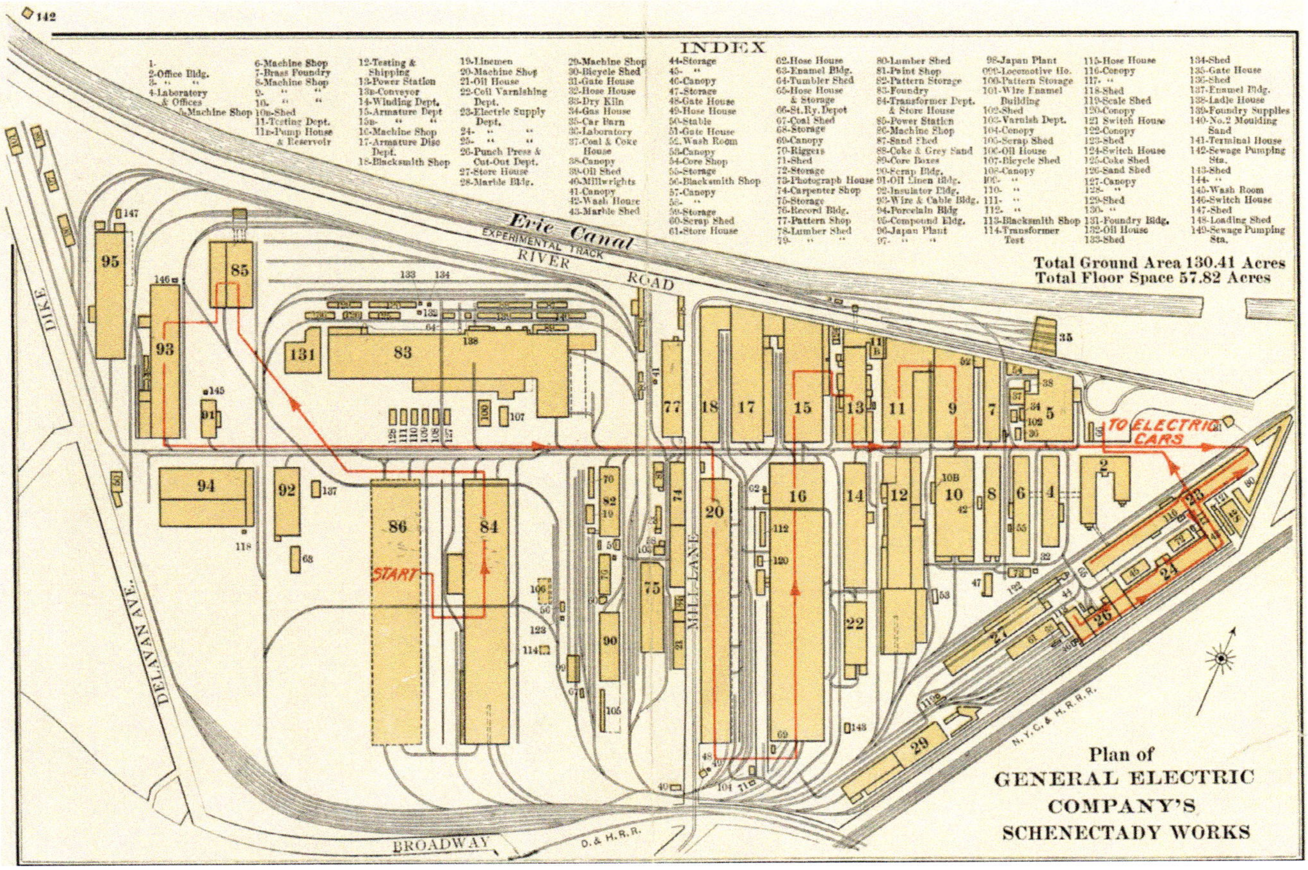

Above: Plan of General Electric Schenectady Works, 1904, showing the trolley loop at the main gate and street railway trackage through Mill Lane. (*American Institute of Electrical Engineers, Schenectady County Public Library*)

Right: Routes of Schenectady Railway, 1899 (total length: 6.2 miles). (*Map by author*)

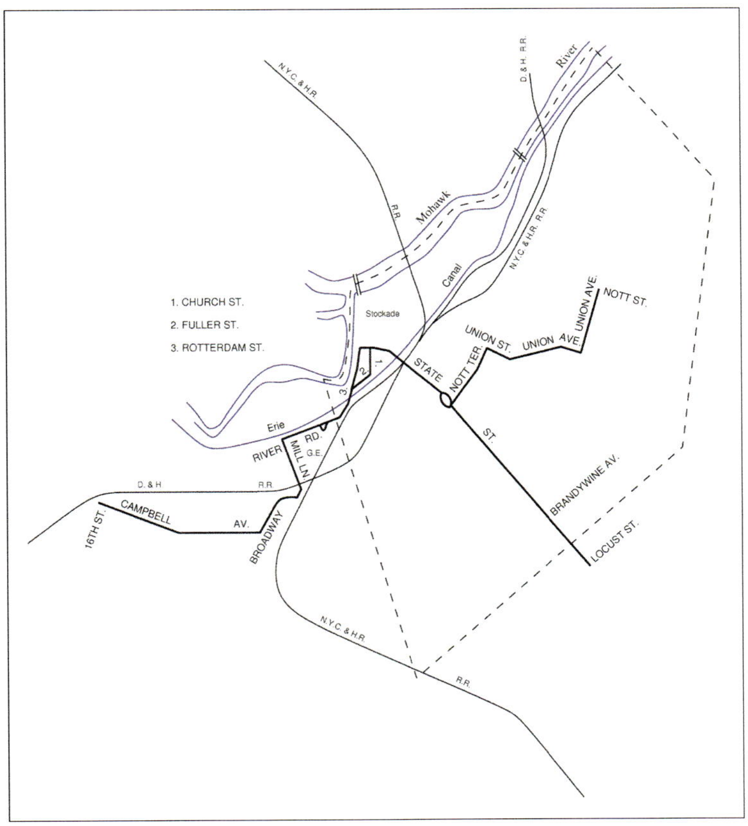

4

Rapid Expansion
(1900–1903)

Although access to the G.E. Realty Plot was built expeditiously, the Schenectady Railway was not by any means neglecting the rest of the city. In 1900, the railway began a rapid expansion of the street railway network that would reach most of the neighborhoods in the city. Two new branches were authorized that year: Albany Street, from Crescent Park past the city line to Elm Street, then Elm Street, from Albany Street to State Street (1.2 miles), and Lafayette Street and Park Place, from State Street to Nott Street (0.8 miles).

In 1901, Schenectady Railway received authorization from the city council to construct or extend six more routes:

1. South Center Street (now Broadway), from State Street to Broadway and the existing Bellevue line (1.1 miles)
2. Nott Street and Van Vranken Avenue, extending the Lafayette Street/Park Place branch to the city line (1.7 miles)
3. Washington Avenue, from State Street to the Mohawk Bridge (rebuilding trackage that was abandoned in 1894) (0.2 miles)
4. Crane Street and Christler Avenue, from South Center Street to the city line (part of this route was in Rotterdam) (1.5 miles)
5. Craig Street, from State Street to Christler Avenue (1.1 miles)
6. McClellan Street, from State Street to Union Street (0.9 miles)

The Schenectady Railway company also had franchises along Union Avenue East (now Rugby Road) that were obtained from the Schenectady Realty Company within both the G.E. Realty Plot and the adjoining Briggs Plot to the east. These franchises remained in effect as the right-of-way for the new street was conveyed to the city. This new line was 0.8 miles in length and joined the McClellan Street line at Union Street, completing a loop with the trackage on Nott Terrace, Union Avenue, and State Street.

The South Center Street line faced some opposition. The first block of South Center Street south of State Street was (and still is) fairly narrow, raising questions about safety and congestion. The franchise therefore specifically restricted the railway to a single track through this block.[1] The mayor initially vetoed approval of this franchise over concerns that the street railway company would stop running trolleys over the grade crossing of the railroad on State Street and thus deprive adequate service to lower State Street, as a primary purpose of the South Center Street trackage was to reroute Bellevue cars directly to downtown. However, after hearing a statement from Schenectady Railway about the company's intent to maintain service across the grade crossing to lower State Street and the G.E. Works, the mayor withdrew his veto.

The trackage on Washington Avenue was part of a planned route across the river, as Scotia also granted Schenectady Railway a franchise in 1901. This route opened for service on April 15, 1902, following the river dyke (now Schonowee Avenue) and Mohawk Avenue to Eagle Street. The total length of the new route was 1.6 miles: 0.2 miles on Washington Avenue in Schenectady, 0.2 miles across the bridge, 0.7 miles along the river dyke and Mohawk Avenue to the center of Scotia (junction of Mohawk and Ballston Avenues), and 0.5 miles further west on Mohawk Avenue to Eagle Street.

A 2018 view of the Briggs Plot. This photo was taken looking north down Parkwood Boulevard at Rugby Road. Though not as exclusive as the G.E. Realty Plot to the west, the Briggs Plot had some extra-wide streets, and a franchise for the street railway on Rugby Road was included in the development. (*Photography by Robert Emerson*)

A 2018 view of the Briggs Plot, located to the east of the G.E. Realty Plot. This photo was taken looking east down Rugby Road at Parkwood Boulevard. Streetcars once ran up and down this street. (*Photography by Robert Emerson*)

The river dyke on the Scotia side of the Mohawk River, with the Washington Avenue bridge in the background. (*From the collection of the Efner History Center at City Hall, Schenectady*)

Service was also extended out Van Vranken Avenue past the city line on a roadside right-of-way 1.6 miles long to the hamlet of Aqueduct on August 23, 1902.

A new 0.9-mile extension on Broadway in the Bellevue neighborhood began partial service on November 12, 1902. The occasion for the opening was a weekend festival called the "Carnival of Months" at the Bellevue Reformed Church. The line began full operation on December 7, 1902, and quickly became the primary route serving Bellevue. Service on Campbell Avenue was retained, though passengers were required to transfer at the junction with the Broadway line at times.

The year 1902 also saw the approval of two further extensions in Schenectady: East Union Street, from McClellan Street to the city line (0.7 miles), and a Nott Street extension of the Union Avenue line, from Wendell Avenue and Nott Street westward along Nott Street and Hattie Place to Van Vranken Avenue (0.4 miles). Other approvals were given to adding a second track on Nott Terrace and Mill Lane. With the exception of the Crane Street, Christler Avenue, and Craig Street routes, all of the above routes would be in operation by 1903.

The city itself also expanded along with the trolley network. In 1902, the Mont Pleasant and Bellevue neighborhoods were annexed by the city and became the Ninth and Tenth Wards respectively.[2] By this time, trackage on State Street had been extended 0.4 miles to the new city line at Elbert Street and beyond, as will be seen in the next chapter.

Belt-line service was started on September 16, 1902, with the "A" Belt and "B" Belt routes. Starting from the G.E. Works, "A" Belt cars proceeded eastward on State Street to the intersection with Nott Terrace. From there, they followed the loop on Nott Terrace, Union Street, Union Avenue, Rugby Road, McClellan Street, and State Street back to Crescent Park and the G.E. Works. "B" Belt cars also started from G.E. and traversed the same loop but in the opposite direction (State Street, McClellan Street, Rugby Road, Union Avenue, Union Street, and Nott Terrace). Service frequency was initially fifteen minutes in each direction. These routes were a hallmark of Schenectady Railway city service for most of the trolley era;

though the railway company experimented with the elimination of these routes a couple of times, the belt routes were reinstated pretty quickly each time because of high customer demand for them.

The single track on Albany Street and the double track on State Street formed a major transportation corridor for the city. Albany Street generally carried the outbound Albany interurbans in addition to the outbound Albany Street cars, while the outbound Troy interurbans, "B" Belt, and State Street cars all used State Street. All of these routes used the inbound track on State Street when returning into Schenectady.

The large expansion created a need for additional car storage and repair facilities, and therefore another new car house and repair shop opened on McClellan Street on February 16, 1903. All repair functions were moved to McClellan Street at this time. Substantial additions were made at Fuller Street as well, including a freight depot and improved amenities for employees such as billiard tables and bowling alleys.

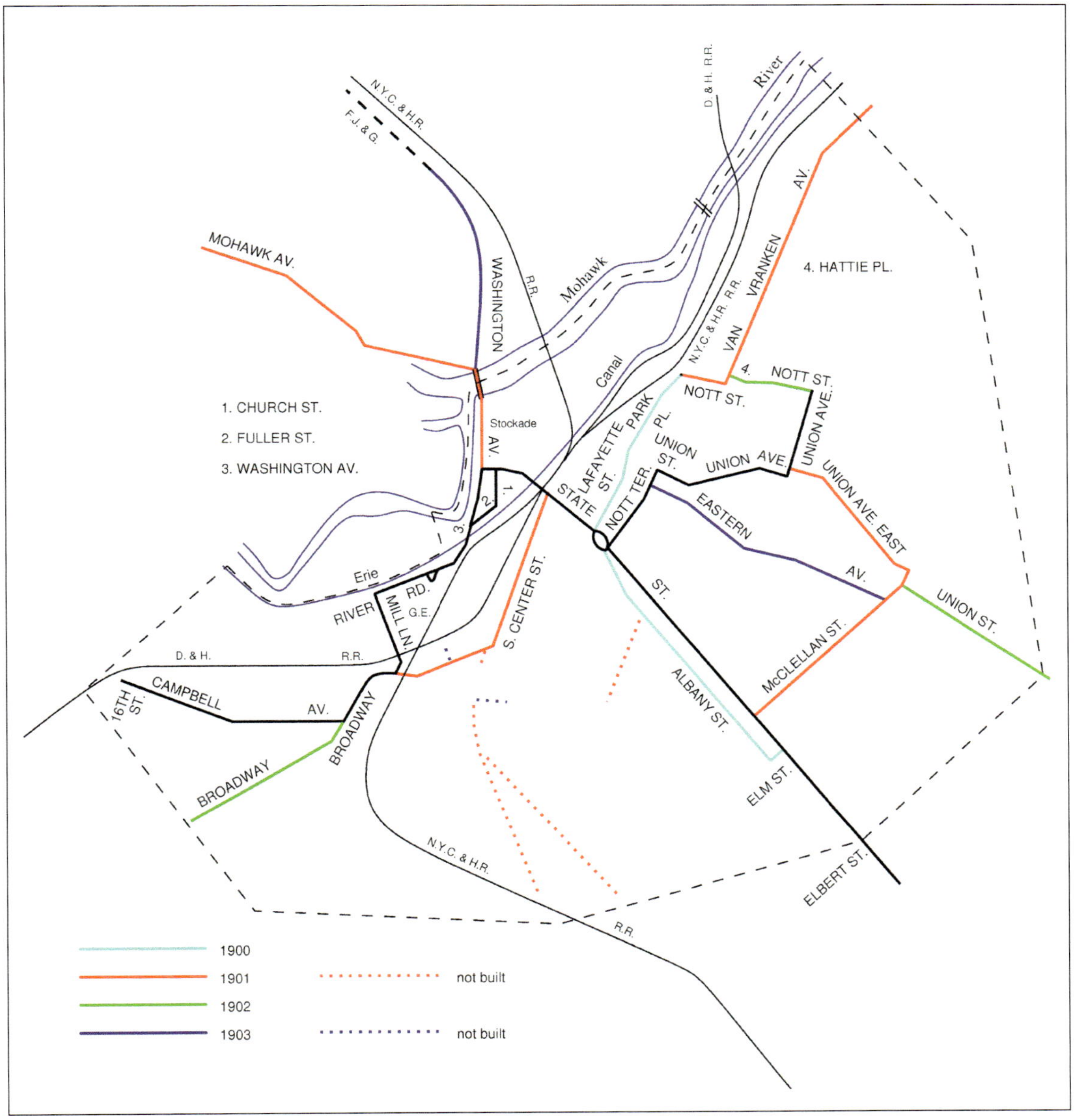

Franchises approved for Schenectady Railway in Schenectady and Scotia, 1900–03. (*Map by author*)

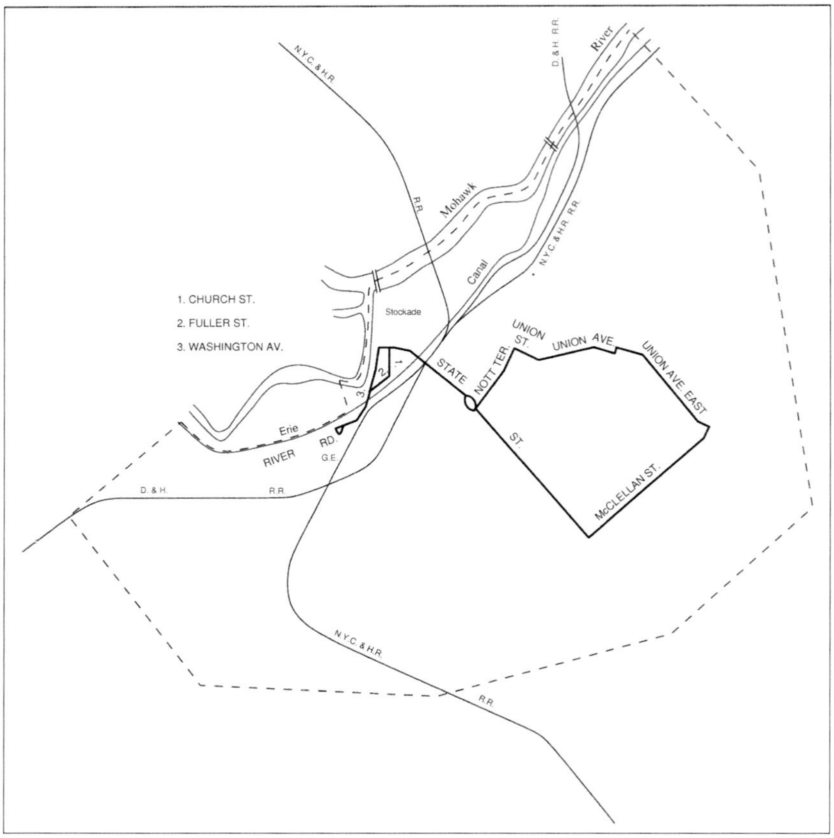

Belt Line routes of Schenectady Railway, 1902. (*Map by author*)

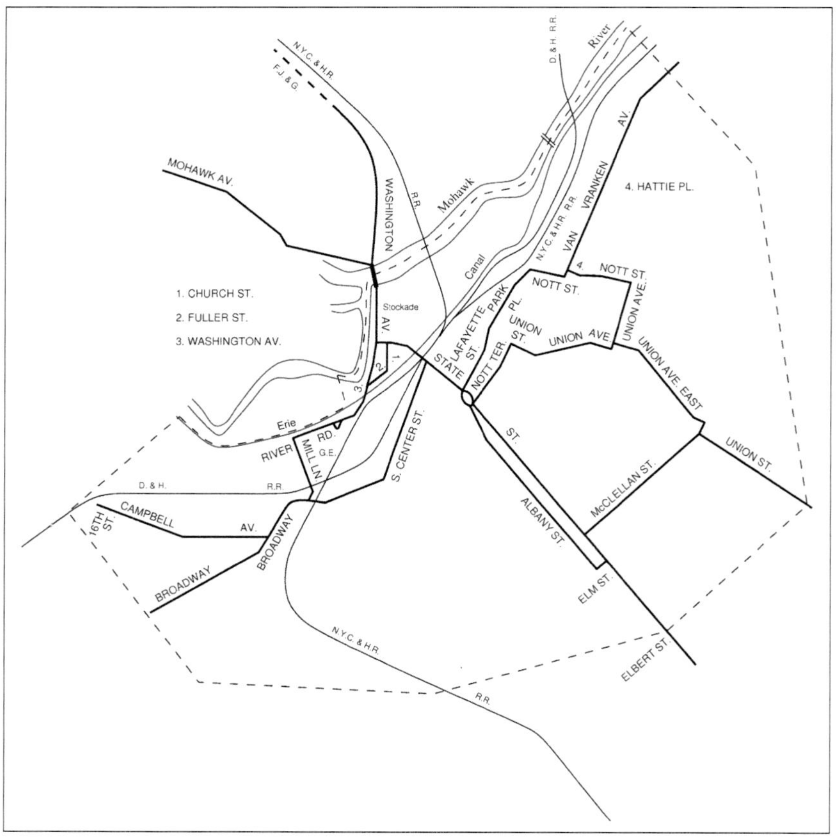

Routes of Schenectady Railway in Schenectady (total length: 15.5 miles) and Scotia (total length: 1.2 miles), 1903. (*Map by author*)

5

The Interurbans
(1901–1907)

While the bulk of Schenectady Railway's patronage was on the local city lines, the company is best remembered today for its interurban runs. These lines made Schenectady the hub of an interurban rail network that linked the major cities of the Capital District.

5.1 Albany

In 1901, Schenectady Railway bid for and won a franchise in Albany for a street railway 0.7 miles in length on Central Avenue, from Watervliet Avenue westward to the city line. This action marked Schenectady Railway's transition from an urban transportation company to a regional interurban carrier, and Albany was a logical initial objective. The company built a 9.8-mile double-track electric railroad from the end of the State Street line to Albany on a roadside right-of-way along the south side of the Albany and Schenectady Turnpike.[1] There, the route followed the newly franchised section of Central Avenue and linked with United Traction rails at Watervliet Avenue. Service between Albany and Schenectady began on September 9, 1901.

Eastbound from Schenectady, the interurbans followed Albany and Elm Streets east to State Street. The interurbans then continued east on State Street and the interurban right-of-way to Albany, following Central Avenue, Washington Avenue, and State Street to the junction of State Street and Broadway. The final 2.5 miles of the trip were over the tracks of United Traction. Westbound from Albany, the interurbans followed State Street, Washington Avenue, and Central Avenue in Albany to the interurban right-of-way. Upon entering Schenectady, the interurbans followed State Street directly to downtown. Once out of the city, the interurban cars were capable of running at 60 mph.

The fare between the two cities was 25 cents, with a discounted rate of 40 cents for a round trip. For intermediate destinations, five fare zones were established, with a fare of 5 cents for each zone or portion of a zone traveled. A schedule was published on October 1 showing half-hourly departures between 5.45 a.m. and 11.15 p.m. from Schenectady and between 6.45 a.m. and 12.15 a.m. from Albany. Tickets were sold at Cherry's News Room, located at 404 State Street, which became a temporary downtown station and waiting room for Schenectady Railway interurban service.

A year later (October 1, 1902), Schenectady Railway opened a new waiting room and office building at 420 State Street. By this time, cars ran between Schenectady and Albany every fifteen minutes during rush hours and afternoons, and overnight service was running every two hours. Hourly express cars (parlor cars), making no stops between Schenectady and Albany, were added in November 1902. The scheduled time for the express trip between the downtown terminals was forty-five minutes.

Starting in September 1903, the intermediate stops on the interurban line were assigned numbers to aid passengers in their identification. These numbers would become well known by area residents over the years and would be widely used

K UPON GUARD PRESIDENT'S TOMB

o Have Been An Attempt to he Vault—May Have Been ped Prisoners from Jail.

N, Ohio, Sept. 30.—A sensa- y of an attempt to blow up the resident McKinley has been in here all the morning and has ch excitement.

d on duty at the tomb to fire a shot at what he took owler about the vault, but, his weapon was diverted, he other prowler who came from ction and struck the rifle, at time thrusting a knife at the bdomen and penetrating his d blouse.

has been astir all day over on the guard at the presi- in Westlawn cemetery. All s to solve the motive for the pen the mystery and the con- at is unanimously drawn by have investigated is that the is true in detail and was a ttempt to blow the vault to

e solution of the mystery is n this: Eight men escaped county jail shortly after 7 t evening. Some of these ave gone into hiding in the and seeing the sentry s tion took desperate chances to get his gun from him defend themselves from prob- ers who were scouring the r the prisoners. But this outed as not probable by ave looked into the matter. gun of the soldier was not

President's Sunday.

GTON, Sept. 30.—President attended divine services at Reformed church, his chosen orship, accompanied by his Ethel and his son Kermit. building was even more an a week ago when Mr. irst appeared there as presi- y pew was filled, and chairs in the aisles and about the room. A knot of people col- side the door, and several

NEW YORK CENTRAL

& HUDSON RIVER R.R

THE FOUR-TRACK TRUNK LINE

The magnificently equipped passenger trains daily travers the Empire State between New York and Buffalo.

This is the only line landing passengers in the City of New York, all trains arrive at and departing from Grand Central Station, Fourth avenue and 42d [illegible] very center of the city.

A. E. BRAINARD, General Agent, Albany, N. Y.
GEORGE H. DANIELS, General Passenger Agent.
P. S. BLODGETT, General Superintendent, New York City.

On and after [illegible] June 16, 1901, trains leave Schenectady as follows:

GOING EAST.

No. [illegible], Accommodation ... 1:45 A. M.
" [illegible], Atlantic Express ... 2:18 "
" 68, Utica Accommodation ... 7:28 "
" *10, Chicago & Boston Spec. ... 8:31 "
" *64, Oneida Accommodation ... 9:37 "
" [illegible] Eng. Exp. ... 10:45 "
" *56, Accommodation ... 12:07 P. M.
" [illegible] ... 1:33 "
" *22, †Lake Shore Limited ... 2:35 "
" 62, Accommodation ... 3:59 "
" [illegible] ... 4:14 "
" *66, Accommodation ... 5:59 "
" 52, Adirondack & Montreal Express ... 6:14 "
" 72, Accommodation ... 7:10 "
" *74, Accommodation ... 9:48 "
" *28, N. Y. & Boston Exp. ... 11:25 "
No. *32, Fast Mail, carries sleeping car passengers only ... 11:50 "

† The New York and Chicago Limited stops to land passengers from Buffalo and points west and to take on passengers for New York.

GOING WEST.

No. *37, Pacific Express ... 2:27 A. M.
" 41, Accommodation ... 7:38 "
" *43, Buffalo Local ... 8:46 "
" *63, Accommodation ... 9:53 "
" 53, Adirondack & Montreal Express ... 11:46 "
" 65, Accommodation ... 11:50 "
" 13, Exposition Express ... 1.51 P. M.
" *45, Syracuse Express ... 2:00
" 7, Day Express ... 3:15 "
" *47, N. Y. & Syracuse Accom ... 5:20 "
" 21, N. Y. & Chicago Exp. ... 6:15 "
" 67, Oneida Express ... 8:27 "
" *23, Western Express ... 10:32 "
" *71, Accommodation ... 11:09
No. 29, Pan. Am. Express ... 11:51 "

Troy Division.

Trains Leave For Troy.

No. *846, Accommodation ... 6:45 A. M.
" 868, Accommodation ... 8:35 "
" 856, Accommodation ... 12:20 P. M.
" 802, Express ... 1:35 "
" 814, Accommodation ... 4:26 "
" 866, Accommodation ... 6:10 "

SCHENECTADY RAILWAY CO.

Albany Division.

Cars leave Schenectady for Albany from corner State and South Centre streets via Albany street at 5:45 a. m., then every half hour until 11:15 p. m., stopping to take on passengers at Summit avenue, Hulett, Martin, Steuben and Swan streets, Brandywine avenue and Kelton avenue.

Returning leave Albany, corner State street and Broadway, at 6:45 a. m., then every half hour until 12:15 a. m.

Tickets for Albany, one way or round trip, can be purchased at Cherry's News Room, near South Centre street, also from Conductors on local cars.

Transfers from local lines given with Albany tickets.

This time table subject to change without notice.

Ballston Lake Farm Property.

Genuine Bargains in desirable Lake Fronts on either side of the Lake. All kinds of Bargains in Farm and Residence Property in the Town of Ballston and on Ballston Lake.

Terms Easy.
Inquire of or address
CHAS. C. EGAN,
Ballston Lake, N. Y.

ASK Druggist for 10 Cent Trial Size

CATARRH

Ely's Cream Balm

Gives Relief at Once

It cleanses, soothes and heals the diseased membrane. It cures catarrh and drives away a cold in the head quickly. It is absorbed. Heals and protects the Membrane. Restores the Senses of Taste and Smell. Full size 5 c.; Trial Size 10c; at druggists or by mail.
ELY BROTHERS, 56 Warren Street, New York.

HAY FEVER

Left: Schenectady Railway interurban schedule, October 1, 1901. (*Daily Union, Schenectady County Public Library*)

Below: Looking southeast down State Street toward Albany from the intersection with Yale Street. This location was outside the city limits of Schenectady when the railway was constructed in 1901, and hence the railway is located on a roadside right-of-way here. (*From the collection of the Efner History Center at City Hall, Schenectady*)

as the names of locations; the following are the stops on the Albany interurban, as listed in *Daily Union*, September 1, 1903 (*: limit of fare zone):

1	Edward Street, city limit	19	Cheavalley's
2	National park	20	White's Road
3	Hastings	21	Temperance Hall
4	Van Zandt's	22	The Elms
5	Green House	23	Lawn House *
6	Stanford's *	24	Cemetery
7	Fagan's	25	Waldorf's
8	Dennick's	26	Mountain View
9	Uplands	27	Lockrow's
10	Ostorm's	28	Dobb's
11	Lisha's Kill church	29	Roessleville
12	Lisha's Kill Store	30	McNutt's
13	Spoor's	31	Culvert (dead stop)
14	Van Hoesen's *	32	Culvert
15	Garrison's	33	City Line *
16	Sub-station	34	Schaffer's Hotel
17	Karner's	35	Vigar's
18	Brown's	36	Watervliet Avenue

5.2 Troy

The next interurban line built by Schenectady Railway was to Troy. Much like the Albany interurban, a double-track route was constructed on a roadside right-of-way for 9.7 miles along the south side of the Troy and Schenectady Turnpike eastward from the Schenectady city line. The route then continued on a separate right-of-way for 1.4 miles to traverse the hill down into Watervliet. In Watervliet, Schenectady Railway built trackage on 1.15 miles of streets to reach the intersection of 25th Street and 3rd Avenue, where it linked with United Traction. Service between Watervliet and Schenectady started on November 15, 1902, though it was interrupted the next day when Watervliet officials blocked the line after determining that the paving job by the railway on 19th Street did not meet the terms of the franchise. After a couple of days, Schenectady Railway agreed to fix the pavement, and service was allowed to resume. The one-way fare from Schenectady to Watervliet was 20 cents.

Starting March 2, 1903, the Schenectady Railway cars ran all the way to Troy Union Station. The fare from Schenectady to Troy was 25 cents. Eastbound from Schenectady, the interurbans followed State Street east to McClellan Street, then traveled on McClellan Street and Union Street to the right-of-way toward Troy. Upon entering Watervliet, the cars followed 12th Avenue, 19th Street, 6th Avenue, and 25th Street. Upon crossing 3rd Avenue, the cars entered United Traction rails and continued on 25th Street and Albany Avenue to the Green Island Bridge. After entering Troy, the cars followed Federal Street, River Street, 3rd Street, and Broadway to Union Station. Westbound, the interurban cars followed Fulton Street and 4th Street to River Street and then retraced the eastbound route back to downtown Schenectady. The scheduled time to complete this route was one hour and eight minutes each way.[2] Cars departed at fifteen-minute intervals throughout the day. The following are the stops on the Troy interurban, as listed in *Daily Union*, September 1, 1903:

1	P. Sweeny	6	Cemetery	11	St. David's Lane
2	R. Van Vranken	7	Irving's	12	Vedder's
3	Maney's	8	Ball Town Road	13	F. Mesick's
4	Livingston Avenue	9	Golf Grounds	14	Carpenter's
5	Chapel	10	Rosendale Road	15	Steel Bridge

16 C. Mesick's
17 Lisha's Kill Road
18 C. Scarff
19 C. Mark's
20 C. C. Van Vranken's
21 Reformed Church
22 River View Road
23 Niskayuna
24 Orlop's
25 Shaker Road
26 Schaffer's Hotel
27 Van Valkenburg's
28 Hess's Hotel
29 Knadler's Hotel
30 Albany Road
31 The Pines
32 La Due's
33 Seven Oaks
34 Maple Wood
35 Nine Elms
36 Latham's
37 Elm Farm
38 Idle Ways
39 Goodrich's
40 Private Right of Way
41 Boulevard Road
42 Wiswell's
43 Nineteenth Street and Twelfth Avenue

5.3 Gloversville/Johnstown

The third interurban line that reached Schenectady was built by another company, the Fonda, Johnstown and Gloversville (FJ&G) Railroad. FJ&G operated both steam and electric railroads connecting Fonda, Johnstown, and Gloversville. In 1902 and 1903, FJ&G built a high-speed double-track electric railroad from existing trackage at Sulphur Springs Junction (located just south of Johnstown) to Schenectady by way of Amsterdam. Schenectady Railway constructed connecting trackage over a distance of 1.05 miles from the Boston and Maine overpass to the Washington Avenue bridge over the Mohawk River. Although this trackage is shown on Schenectady Railway maps, there does not seem to be any indication that Schenectady Railway ever ran its own service over this section.

Service began on July 1, 1903. FJ&G cars entered Schenectady via Washington Avenue and State Street, looped around Crescent Park, and then started back west on State Street for the return trip. Some FJ&G trips also operated to the G.E. loop. Fares were 70 cents for a one-way trip between Gloversville and Schenectady, with a $1.20 fare for a round trip. From Johnstown, the fares were 60 cents and $1.05 respectively. Service was hourly, with a scheduled travel time of one hour and twenty-four minutes between Schenectady and Gloversville and one hour and eleven minutes between Schenectady and Johnstown.[3]

FJ&G bought eight heavyweight interurban cars numbered 100 to 107 from St. Louis Car Company for this line. Costing $14,000 each, these cars had top-notch amenities for passengers, including restrooms, ice-cooled fountain water, hot water heating, red plush seats, and an interior mahogany finish. As we shall see, this was not the last time that FJ&G would make significant investments in the rolling stock for this line. Four 75-hp motors (GE-73) powered each car, which was capable of averaging 45 mph. Four more identical cars (numbered 150 to 153) were purchased the next year.

FJ&G car no. 103, one of eight purchased for interurban service between Gloversville and Schenectady. (*From the collection of the Efner History Center at City Hall, Schenectady*)

Overall, Schenectady Railway and FJ&G enjoyed a very cooperative relationship, with each company lending equipment to the other in times of need. Both companies also built their electric railways to high standards. In contrast, United Traction refused to allow the FJ&G interurban cars to regularly operate over their rails on account of their heavy weight. FJ&G customers would have to transfer in Schenectady in order to reach Albany throughout the era of electric interurban operation.

5.4 Ballston Spa

Schenectady Railway sought to extend its network to the north as well. This expansion started with a "trolley war" in Ballston Spa. Both Schenectady Railway and the Hudson Valley Railway Company (H.V.R.C.) believed they had a valid franchise to construct a street railway on Front Street, and crews from both companies started working on the same street on the same day—April 18, 1902.[4] After a stoppage of work by both companies and a court battle, H.V.R.C. conceded the right of Schenectady Railway to build on the portion of Front Street that lay west of Bath Street.

To reach Ballston Spa, the company constructed an 11.94-mile route from a junction point on the Aqueduct branch. This route featured a bridge over the Mohawk River just west of Aqueduct. This bridge was reportedly the longest trolley bridge in the world and was built in sections to limit potential damage caused by river ice in the winter. From the north end of the bridge, a double-track electric railroad was constructed on private right-of-way northward through Alplaus all the way to Ballston Spa. Much of the right-of-way paralleled the D&H railroad tracks that ran north from Schenectady to Saratoga Springs.[5]

Service to Ballston from Schenectady began on June 30, 1904, with cars traveling from downtown up the Lafayette Street and Van Vranken Avenue line past the city limits. At Aqueduct Junction (0.9 miles from the city line), the cars entered the new trackage over the Mohawk River bridge and the right-of-way to Ballston Spa. The trackage entered

Schenectady Railway bridge over the Mohawk River near Aqueduct. Dubbed "the longest trolley bridge in the world," this bridge was constructed as part of the Ballston Spa line, which opened in 1904. The arches of the Erie Canal aqueduct at Aqueduct can be seen downstream. (*From the collection of the Efner History Center at City Hall, Schenectady*)

Ballston Spa over Charlton Street and Front Street, terminating at Bath Street. Passengers could transfer there to Hudson Valley Railway cars to reach Saratoga Springs. A waiting room for both Schenectady Railway and H.V.R.C. passengers opened on the southeast corner of Bath and Front Streets (55 Front Street). A 25-cent fare was established for a one-way trip from Schenectady to Ballston Spa. The schedule time from downtown Schenectady was about fifty minutes.[6]

Schenectady Railway opened a new park concurrently with the Ballston line: Forest Park. Located at the southern end of Ballston Lake, Forest Park had facilities similar to Brandywine Park and was accessed by a stop on the new Ballston interurban line. "Twilight specials" operated on summer weekends to the park, generally departing downtown Schenectady around 8 p.m. and starting their return trip from the park at 10.30 p.m.

A branch line 0.7 miles in length from Alplaus to Rexford was also built, with direct service to and from downtown Schenectady. In 1906, Luna Park was opened in Rexford, offering another recreation option for area residents. Unlike Forest Park, Luna Park was not owned by the railway.

Like most street railway companies of the time, Schenectady Railway had a diverse collection of rolling stock to serve passengers. Six interurban cars (numbered 606 to 611) built by Jones in 1904 were the premier cars in the fleet. They were principally used on the Ballston line. These cars boasted a mahogany interior and a top speed of 70 mph.

Above left: This store at 55 Front Street in Ballston Spa served as a waiting room for H.V.R.C. and Schenectady Railway passengers for several years. Bath Street was the dividing line between the franchises of the two companies, and many passengers transferred here to travel to and from Saratoga Springs after the Ballston line opened in 1904. The Ballston Spa stop for Schenectady Railway later moved to Main Street and Malta Avenue, 0.2 miles up the line. (*Photography by Robert Emerson*)

Above right: Another 2018 view of the former H.V.R.C./Schenectady Railway waiting room at 55 Front Street in Ballston Spa. (*Photography by Robert Emerson*)

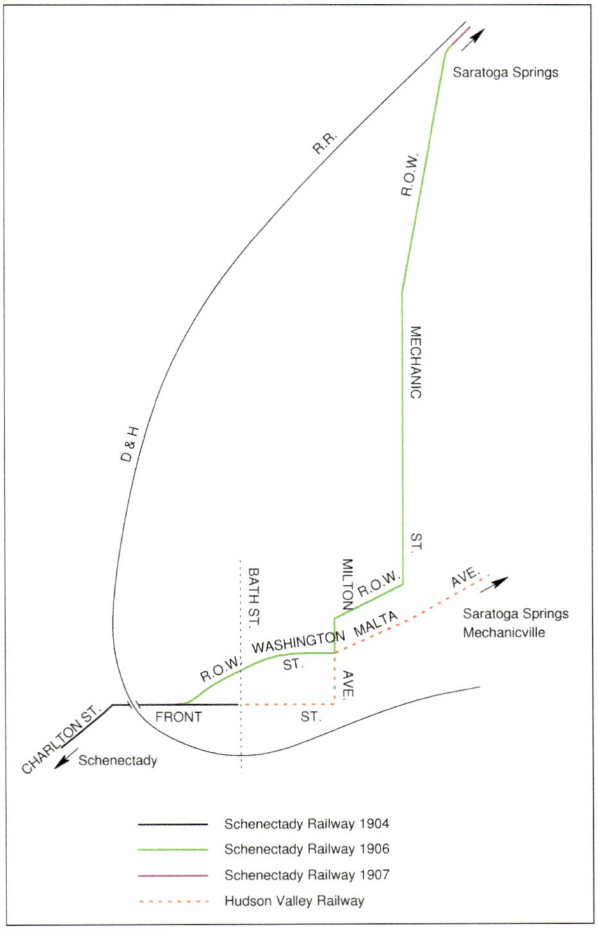

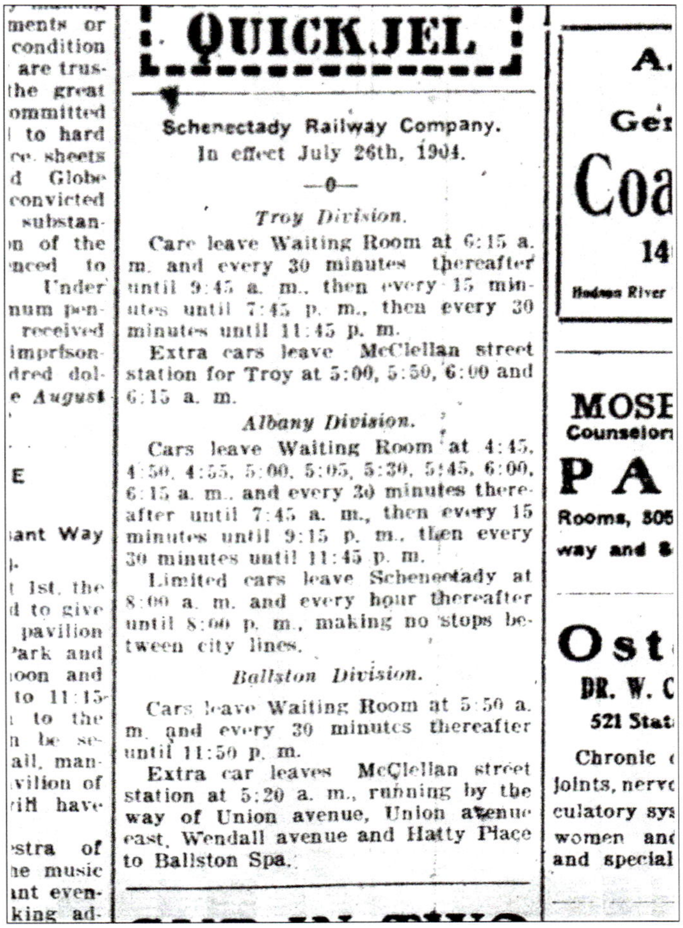

QUICKJEL

Schenectady Railway Company.
In effect July 26th, 1904.

—0—

Troy Division.

Cars leave Waiting Room at 6:15 a. m. and every 30 minutes thereafter until 9:45 a. m., then every 15 minutes until 7:45 p. m., then every 30 minutes until 11:45 p. m.

Extra cars leave McClellan street station for Troy at 5:00, 5:50, 6:00 and 6:15 a. m.

Albany Division.

Cars leave Waiting Room at 4:45, 4:50, 4:55, 5:00, 5:05, 5:30, 5:45, 6:00, 6:15 a. m., and every 30 minutes thereafter until 7:45 a. m., then every 15 minutes until 9:15 p. m., then every 30 minutes until 11:45 p. m.

Limited cars leave Schenectady at 8:00 a. m. and every hour thereafter until 8:00 p. m., making no stops between city lines.

Ballston Division.

Cars leave Waiting Room at 5:50 a. m. and every 30 minutes thereafter until 11:50 p. m.

Extra car leaves McClellan street station at 5:20 a. m., running by the way of Union avenue, Union avenue east, Wendall avenue and Hatty Place to Ballston Spa.

Above left: Street railway trackage in Ballston Spa, 1904–07. (*Map by author*)

Above right: Schenectady Railway interurban schedule, July 26, 1904. (*Schenectady Gazette, Schenectady County Public Library*)

Schenectady Railway car no. 608, one of six purchased for interurban service between Schenectady and Ballston Spa. (*From the collection of the Efner History Center at City Hall, Schenectady*)

5.5 Saratoga Springs

Saratoga Springs was a premier resort in the early twentieth century, and Schenectady Railway did not lose sight of the goal of reaching the city directly. With a continuation on Front Street blocked by H.V.R.C., Schenectady Railway began assembling a new route to reach Saratoga. The company acquired land in 1905 on the north side of Front Street to build new track on a short stretch of private right-of-way down a slope to Washington Street. The route was continued on Washington Street to Milton Avenue near the center of town and extended northward through Ballston Spa on Milton Avenue, Mechanic Street, and private rights-of-way to a junction with the D&H railroad. Service over this route began operating in 1906, with passengers now being able to transfer to D&H trains at the junction (named Ballston Junction).[7]

The company was not done with construction, however. Schenectady Railway leased 5.55 miles of right-of-way alongside the D&H steam railroad tracks north from Ballston Junction. Two tracks with overhead wire were constructed over this leased right-of-way. The goal of direct service to Saratoga Springs was finally achieved on July 2, 1907, when Schenectady Railway cars began regular service between Schenectady and Saratoga Springs using this trackage. Schenectady Railway cars used the H.V.R.C. terminal at the corner of Broadway and Congress Streets.[8] The fare from Schenectady to Saratoga Springs was 40 cents. Service was generally hourly, with one hour and ten minutes scheduled for the trip between downtown Schenectady and Saratoga Springs.[9] This route became the premier route for Schenectady Railway. The "best" rolling stock was generally assigned to the Saratoga service.

"Capital Limited" service from Albany to Saratoga Springs via Schenectady was initiated on July 27 of the following year (1908). Cars departed Albany hourly from 8 a.m. to 7 p.m., making only four intermediate stops on the way to Saratoga: Schenectady, Ballston Lake, Forest Park, and Ballston Spa. The trip time was one hour and forty-five minutes. Schenectady Railway issued a brochure titled "Trolley Trips" around this time promoting the many sightseeing attractions in the area and the ability to reach them via the trolleys.

This junction on Front Street in Ballston Spa is where Schenectady Railway's Saratoga extension began. Heading toward Saratoga Springs, the extension branched off to the left of the Ballston Spa line at this location, continued down the slope seen in this image, and then followed Washington Street to Lincoln Corner. *(From the collection of the Efner History Center at City Hall, Schenectady)*

Caricature of Edward F. Peck, who was the general manager of Schenectady Railway from 1902 to 1912. (*From the collection of the Efner History Center at City Hall, Schenectady*)

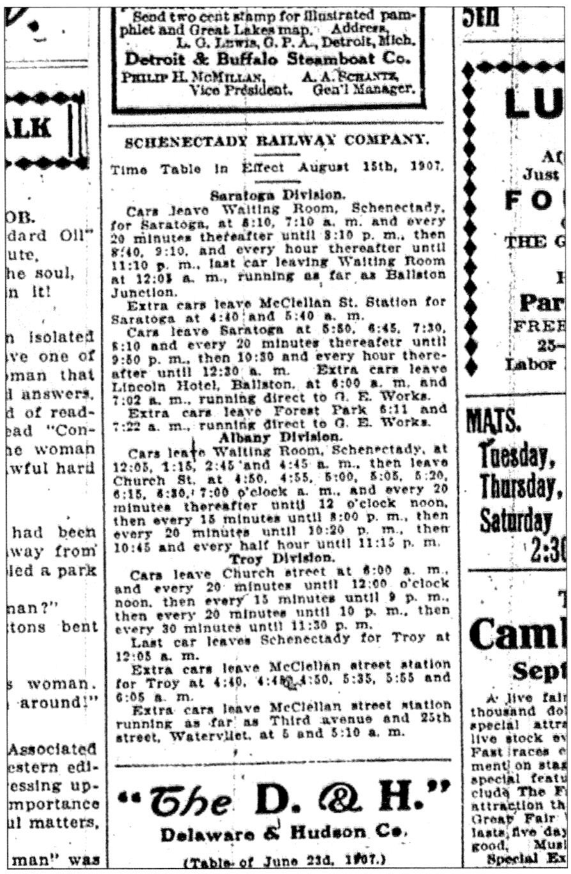

Send two cent stamp for illustrated pamphlet and Great Lakes map. Address,
L. G. Lewis, G. P. A., Detroit, Mich.
Detroit & Buffalo Steamboat Co.
Philip H. McMillan, Vice President. A. A. Schantz, Gen'l Manager.

SCHENECTADY RAILWAY COMPANY.

Time Table in Effect August 15th, 1907.

Saratoga Division.

Cars leave Waiting Room, Schenectady, for Saratoga, at 6:10, 7:10 a. m. and every 20 minutes thereafter until 8:10 p. m., then 8:40, 9:10, and every hour thereafter until 11:10 p. m., last car leaving Waiting Room at 12:05 a. m., running as far as Ballston Junction.

Extra cars leave McClellan St. Station for Saratoga at 4:40 and 5:40 a. m.

Cars leave Saratoga at 5:50, 6:45, 7:30, 8:10 and every 20 minutes thereafetr until 9:50 p. m., then 10:30 and every hour thereafter until 12:30 a. m. Extra cars leave Lincoln Hotel, Ballston, at 6:00 a. m. and 7:02 a. m., running direct to G. E. Works.

Extra cars leave Forest Park 6:11 and 7:22 a. m., running direct to G. E. Works.

Albany Division.

Cars leave Waiting Room, Schenectady, at 12:05, 1:15, 2:45 and 4:45 a. m., then leave Church St. at 4:50, 4:55, 5:00, 5:05, 5:20, 6:15, 6:30, 7:00 o'clock a. m., and every 20 minutes thereafter until 12 o'clock noon, then every 15 minutes until 8:00 p. m., then every 20 minutes until 10:20 p. m., then 10:45 and every half hour until 11:15 p. m.

Troy Division.

Cars leave Church street at 6:00 a. m., and every 20 minutes until 12:00 o'clock noon, then every 15 minutes until 9 p. m., then every 20 minutes until 10 p. m., then every 30 minutes until 11:30 p. m.

Last car leaves Schenectady for Troy at 12:05 a. m.

Extra cars leave McClellan street station for Troy at 4:40, 4:48, 4:50, 5:35, 5:55 and 6:05 a. m.

Extra cars leave McClellan street station running as far as Third avenue and 25th street, Watervliet, at 5 and 5:10 a. m.

"The D. & H."
Delaware & Hudson Co.
(Table of June 23d, 1907.)

Schenectady Railway interurban schedule, August 15, 1907. (*Daily Union, Schenectady County Public Library*)

Routes of Schenectady Railway, c. 1907. (*Author's collection*)

6

Meanwhile, Back in Schenectady (1903–1905)

Though just 1 mile from downtown Schenectady, residents of Mont Pleasant would still not have any trolleys to get there when service to Ballston Spa (16 miles away) started in 1904. Schenectady Railway had acquired franchises on Crane and Craig Streets for accessing Mont Pleasant in 1901, but they proved inadequate for serving the new Ninth Ward. Crane Street climbed a steep slope on unstable soil, so the railway instead sought access to the neighborhood over either Congress Street via the Bellevue line or Craig Street via the Albany Street line. Either route would require a bridge over a steep valley.

In 1903, another route into Mont Pleasant began to take shape, as the city council approved a franchise for street railway operation on Francis Street from Crane Street to Willett Avenue. To complete the route, Schenectady Railway also sought to construct trackage on Hulett and Schenectady Streets in 1903, but the city council postponed approval until 1904, when a franchise was granted for operation on Hulett Street, from State Street to Strong Avenue (0.5 miles), and a 0.5-mile parallel path on Schenectady Street and Strong Avenue, from Albany Street to the intersection of Strong Avenue with Hulett Street. Electric current flowing through a water main on Hulett Street was cited as a particular concern. Schenectady Railway completed construction of a trestle over Cotton Factory Hollow (also known as Pleasant Valley) in 1905, linking Hulett Street and Francis Street and finally enabling direct service to Mont Pleasant. The inaugural run was celebrated on March 31, 1905. Service reached the junction of Crane and Pearl Streets, 0.9 miles from the junction of Strong Avenue and Hulett Street.

Another addition to the network was also authorized by the city council in 1903: E. Liberty Street (now Eastern Avenue), from Nott Terrace to McClellan Street (1.1 miles). This route, however, would take a few years to come to fruition. In the interim, demand for service along outer Union Street was increasing. Initially, this route was served by the Watervliet and Troy interurbans, but after a year and a half, a new city route from downtown to Rosendale Road (stop 10 on the Troy line) was established to improve local service. This route followed Union Avenue and Union Avenue East (Rugby Road) to reach outer Union Street. The Belt Line service, which also used these single-tracked streets, was discontinued. In its place, a companion route over State Street and McClellan Street to the intersection of McClellan and Union Streets was established.

While all of this was going on, General Electric decided to sell its ownership of the local street railway system. In October 1904, Schenectady Railway was purchased by the two major railroads that served Schenectady—the New York Central and the D&H—with each railroad getting a 50 percent stake.

As the Mont Pleasant line neared its long-awaited completion, attention turned back to downtown and a proposal for a joint railroad and streetcar station for the city. With the railroads and the city about to start a major railroad elevation and grade-crossing elimination project, the time was ripe for a grand new railroad depot for both railroads to serve the city, and it made sense to include a streetcar terminal in the plans for the union station. The plan that emerged became known as the "subway" and centered on the placement of streetcar tracks beneath the newly elevated railroad tracks for two blocks. The tracks would be accessed from the north via new trackage on South Avenue, Fonda Street (now Jay Street), and Union Street. On the south end, the "subway" tracks would connect to State Street via a wye arrangement.

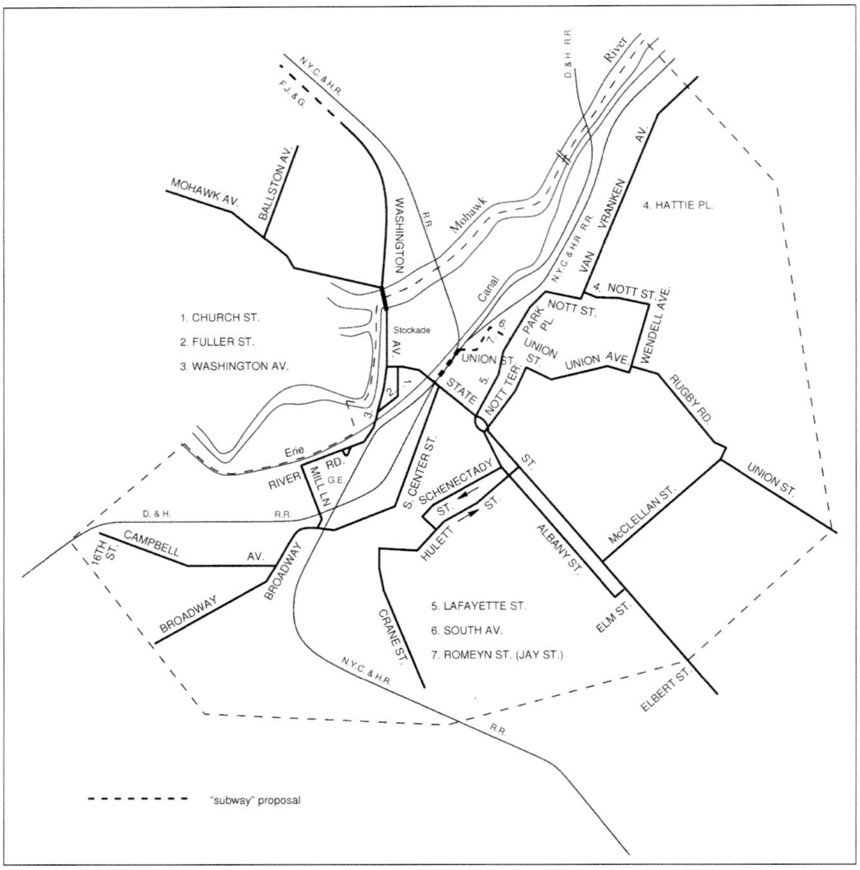

Routes of Schenectady Railway in Schenectady (total length: 17.4 miles) and Scotia (total length: 1.6 miles), 1905. *(Map by author)*

The new union station, which was located on the west side of the tracks between Liberty and State Streets, would include a waiting room, loops, and terminal trackage for streetcar passengers.

This streetcar station was never built, as the city council and the street railway company were unable to come to agreement on the terms of the project. The specific items of contention were numerous but can be grouped into five categories:

1. Physical specifications of portions of the project
2. Cost-sharing for portions of the improvements
3. A requirement to provide uniformed flagmen at the locations where the streetcar tracks cross the sidewalks
4. A waiver of liability for the city
5. A requirement to fix streetcar fares at existing levels

This last requirement may have seemed superfluous as fares were already limited to 5 cents by the existing city franchises, but the railway was offering a discount of six tickets for 25 cents. This particular issue was a harbinger of things to come.

Discussions between Schenectady Railway and representatives of the city council resulted in a draft ordinance which was placed to a vote by the whole council. The vote was 13–8 in favor, but as a two-thirds vote was required for approving public expenditures, the ordinance was not passed. Schenectady Railway stated that they would not make any concessions in addition to those which had already been offered in the draft ordinance. Formally, the ordinance was tabled for future consideration, but no further action was taken.

Having the streetcar tracks cross the sidewalk on the north side of busy State Street created a number of safety concerns and potential disruptions to pedestrian traffic for the businesses in the area; this factor seems to be the biggest reason that a strong consensus never emerged for the "subway" project. The grade crossing elimination project for the railroads was carried out, and a magnificent Beaux-Arts Union Station opened in 1908, but no provisions for a streetcar terminal were included.

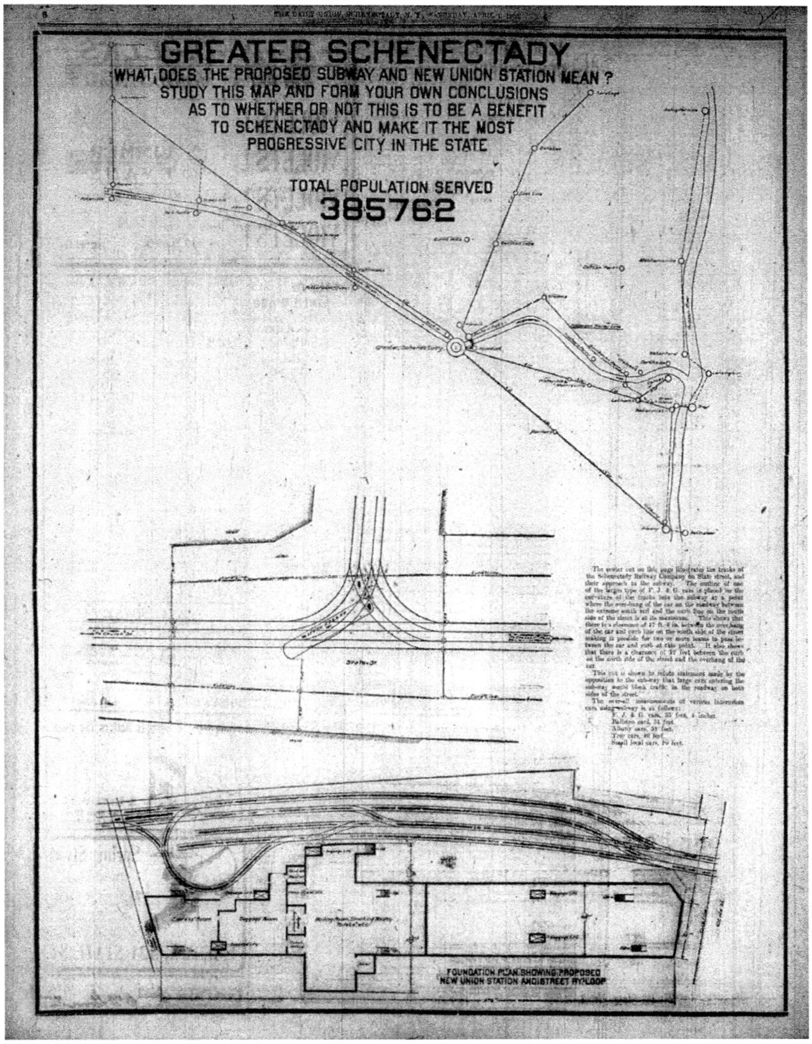

Right: "Subway" proposal. (*Daily Union, Schenectady County Public Library*)

Below: Plan of the union station's ground floor and streetcar terminal under the "subway" proposal. (*Evening Star, Schenectady County Public Library*)

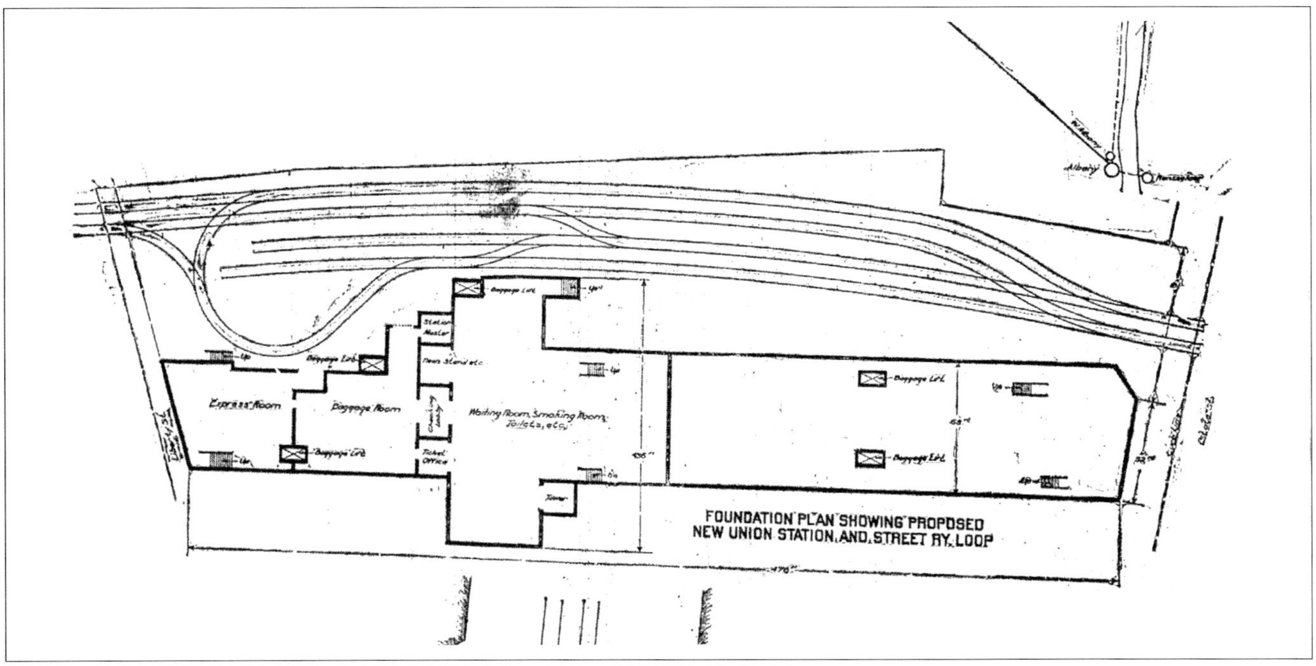

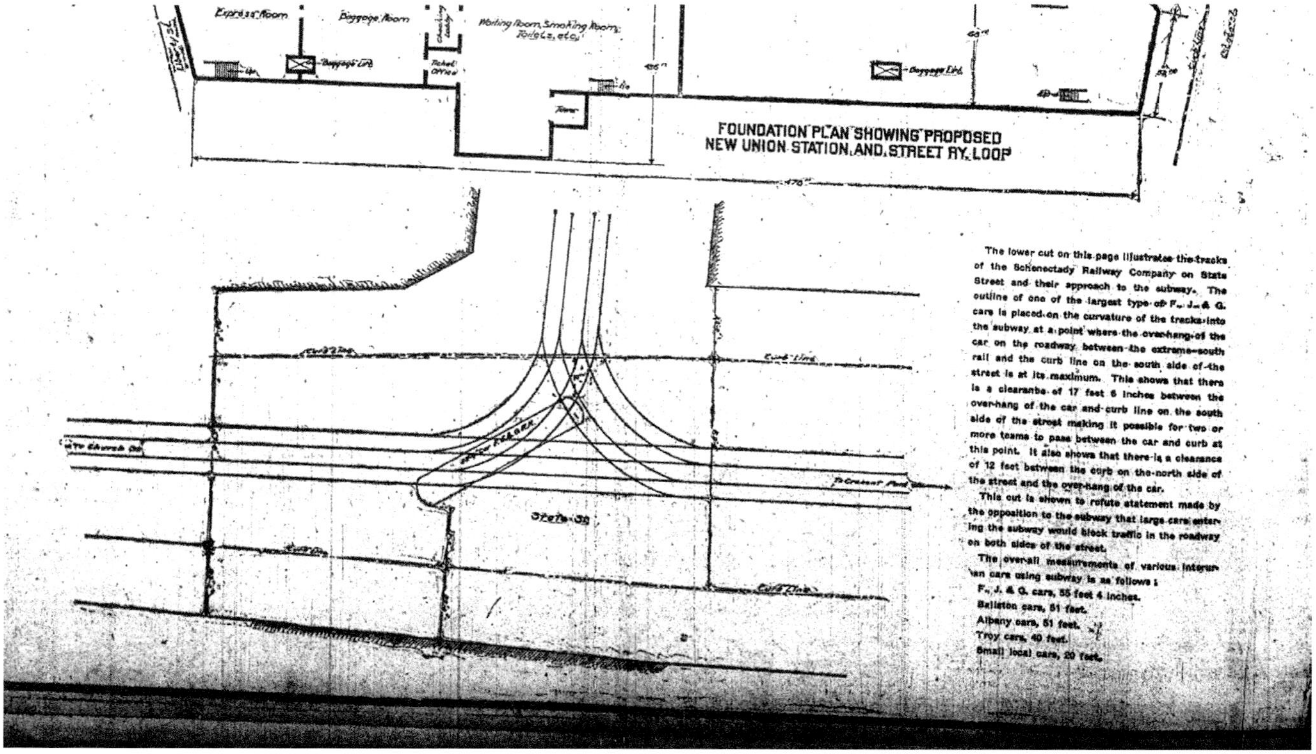

Plan of the trackage and junction in State St. under the "subway" proposal. (*Evening Star, Schenectady County Public Library*)

VIEW OF PROPOSED TROLLEY SUBWAY AND STATE STREET FRONT OF NEW STATION.

"Subway" proposal. (*Evening Star, Schenectady County Public Library*)

7

Gridlock (1905–1911)

All of the growth and street railway construction in the preceding years resulted in a large amount of trolley traffic congestion by 1906. Schenectady was hardly the only city with this problem, though the street pattern, which tended to funnel all traffic into State Street, exacerbated the situation. Narrow side streets with only a single track further compounded the congestion, as streetcars trying to traverse them had to wait in the middle of State Street for the track to clear. Interurban cars also had to switch tracks in the middle of State Street when reversing direction after arrival. The closure of the grade crossing of the D&H at the south end of Mill Lane simply added to the problem.[1]

The traffic gridlock was matched with political gridlock. Whereas relations between Schenectady Railway and Schenectady City Council had been fairly amicable, the difficulties with the "subway" plan were the start of a much more fractious period. The change in ownership of Schenectady Railway added an element of suspicion. Many members of both the city council and the general public were distrustful of "absentee" ownership and management.

The Belt Lines were re-established at the end of 1905 by popular demand. Rosendale Road service was changed to a shuttle on Union Street between McClellan Street and Rosendale Road. The delayed project for laying trackage in Eastern Avenue was finally completed in 1906, permitting Rosendale Road service to run all the way downtown again. The "A" and "B" Belt routes were shifted onto Eastern Avenue shortly afterward, with Rosendale Road cars using Union Avenue and Rugby Road; both Schenectady Railway and its customers found this routing to be preferable. Congestion in downtown remained, however.

A new participant entered the scene during this period. On June 6, 1907, Governor Charles Evans Hughes signed a major overhaul of public utilities regulation in New York State. The act created two five-member Public Service Commissions, with one for the First District (New York City) and the other for the Second District (all of the state outside New York City). Street railroads were one of the utilities covered by the act. Among the requirements of the act for street railways were the following: fares must be "just and reasonable;" a schedule of rates and fares must be filed with the commission; and the commission must approve construction for any new franchise.

In April 1906, Schenectady Railway proposed new trackage on Edison Avenue and Lyon Street for access to the G.E. Works. Action on this proposal was delayed for a year while the city and the railway negotiated a set of track and street improvements. Beside the Edison Avenue franchise, the improvements included new trackage on Smith and Clinton Streets and the laying of double track at a number of locations. In exchange, cession of railway company land on Dock Street for street widening, payment of one-third of the cost of widening the N.Y.C. R.R. culvert on South Center Street, and widening of a 2,500-foot-long stretch of Nott Street (from Park Place to Van Vranken Avenue) by Schenectady Railway were also included in the discussions. The city resolved on April 4, 1907, to include a requirement to make the bulk discount tickets permanent (six tickets for 25 cents), but Schenectady Railway stated politely but firmly that they would not accept this condition. An informal discussion on May 3 yielded an agreement satisfactory to both parties, and the city council ratified franchises for both Edison Avenue and Smith and Clinton Streets on May 28 as part of this agreement.

View looking west down Eastern Avenue toward the city center from Brandywine Avenue, *c.* 1906. The open land seen here would soon be filled with houses to accompany the completion of the trolley tracks and the establishment of Belt Line service on Eastern Avenue. (*From the collection of the Efner History Center at City Hall, Schenectady*)

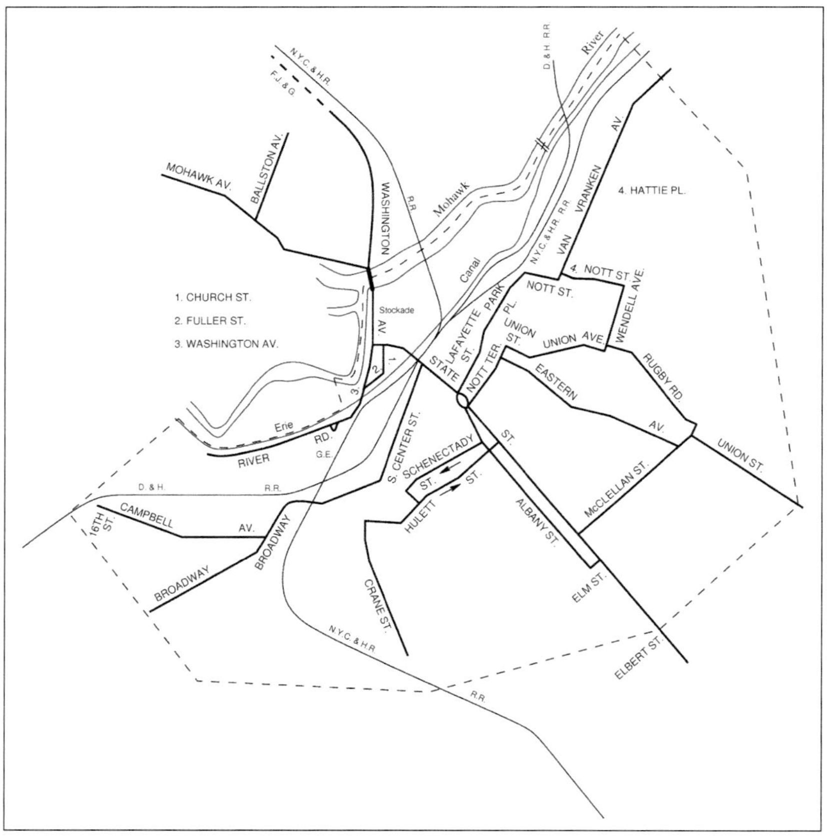

Routes of Schenectady Railway in Schenectady (total length: 18.7 miles) and Scotia (total length: 1.6 miles), 1907. (*Map by author*)

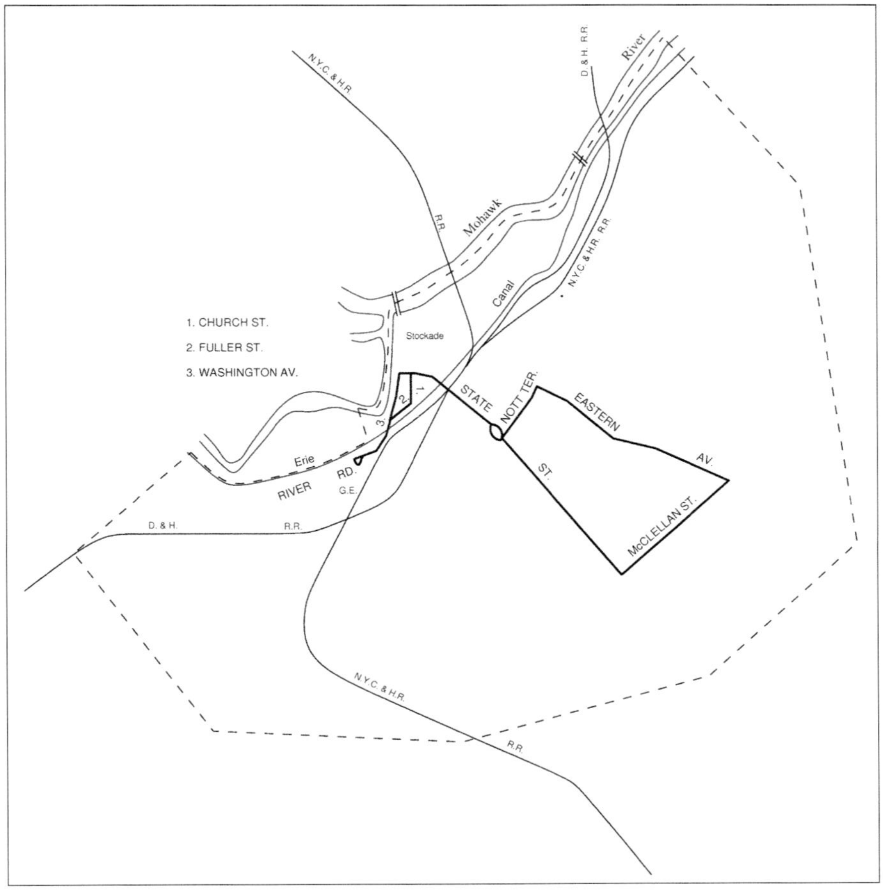

Belt Line routes of Schenectady Railway, 1907.
(Map by author)

The congestion downtown did not improve. Property owners stridently opposed a second track on Center Street between State and Smith Streets due to the narrowness of the street, and hence the city council rejected the necessary franchise modification at a meeting on September 10. Schenectady Railway regarded this rejection as a breach of the agreement between the railway and the city. Schenectady Railway planned to expand the downtown waiting room at 420 State Street with a rear entrance on Smith Street to create a downtown interurban terminal. The railway considered the double-track on Center Street to be the most critical component of the congestion relief plan, and without it, matters ground to a halt. The railway did not exercise the franchise for Smith and Clinton Streets, evidently concluding that without the double track on Center Street, the partial relief afforded by this trackage was not worth the cost, which would include widening Smith Street.

No work was done on Edison Avenue either for a couple of years. A couple of reasons were cited for delaying this work: first, the aforementioned lack of double track on Center Street, which would have enabled trolleys coming from the east on State Street to access the new trackage, and second, the need for General Electric to complete a design for the new entrance plaza that was being constructed at the junction of Washington Avenue and Edison Avenue. As can be seen from the plans of the G.E. works, a number of structures were removed to make room for the plaza. By 1910, Schenectady Railway had finally sought P.S.C. approval for constructing the 0.3-mile route and was laying tracks in Edison Avenue later that year; the street was paved the same year.

Other improvements were also taking place to serve the growing Schenectady Works of General Electric. Although tracks were removed from Mill Lane around 1907, Schenectady Railway retained the tracks on River Road and obtained a franchise to extend them 0.4 miles further west. G.E. built a new shelter at Gate 69-E, located about two-thirds of a mile west of the main entrance and trolley loop. This location became known as "G.E. Terminal," and while most trips to the G.E. Works still terminated at the loop, some runs would continue on River Road to G.E. Terminal. Even FJ&G scheduled a daily trip during rush hours that served the G.E. Terminal stop.

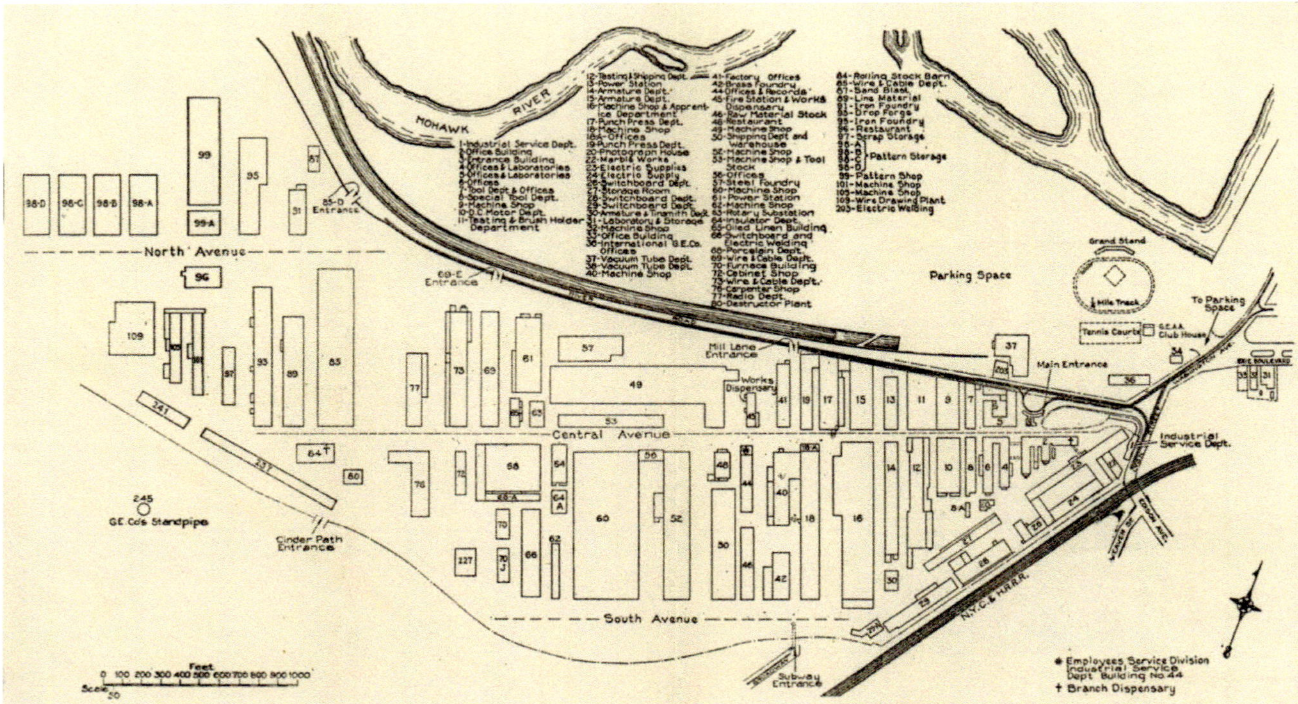

Plan of General Electric Schenectady Works, 1926, showing the closure of Mill Lane as a public street and the extension of the street railway on River Road. (*General Electric, Schenectady County Public Library*)

View looking west down River Road toward the G.E. Terminal stop. The Erie Canal is located to the right. The catenary on the right is for a test track that G.E. built alongside the canal. (*From the collection of the Efner History Center at City Hall, Schenectady*)

Concurrently, Schenectady Railway had to come up with a new plan for downtown. After some time, they found a new location for a suitable downtown station at 512 State Street and a way to serve it without double-tracking Center Street. Essentially, the plan consisted of shifting the new downtown tracks on Center and Clinton Streets, eastward to Clinton Street and Veeder Avenue. The Clinton Street track would then function as the second track for inbound trolleys on Center Street.

Meanwhile, relations with the city council deteriorated further. Schenectady Railway did not carry out the widening of Nott Street where a double track had been laid; this widening was (in the city council's view) part of the agreement reached on May 3, 1907. Schenectady Railway did not submit many petitions during these years, but the Council's distrust of the railway company is palpable. The ending of the sale of the "red tickets" (six for a quarter) in March 1909 added to the animosity, and the council received a number of petitions from taxpayers, civic associations, and organized labor calling for the refusal of any further franchises until sale of the "red tickets" was resumed. Things pretty much reached rock bottom when the council took no apparent action on a petition dated October 24, 1910, for new tracks on Smith Street, Clinton Street, and Veeder Avenue. Mayor Charles Duryee filed a complaint about the streetcar fares with the P.S.C. on December 12, claiming that the discontinuance of the "red tickets" resulted in fares that were "unjust and unreasonable."

In a disappointment to many, the Public Service Commission on April 17, 1911, ruled that it did not have authority under the public service law to order the sale of tickets at a reduced rate. Such tickets did not qualify as commutation tickets as they were valid for use anytime, anywhere. The commission ruled that it could only regulate the maximum fare, which was still 5 cents a ride, though the city was invited to present a follow-up case that 5 cents was no longer "just and reasonable." Meanwhile, matters with Schenectady Railway remained at a standstill. In a letter dated June 2, 1911, the president of the Common Council stated that the railway's petition would receive immediate attention if the railway started selling seven tickets for 25 cents during rush hour and also would purchase the land for widening Nott Street.

The stalemate finally broke on June 12. At that meeting, the Council agreed that the issue of fares should be referred to the Public Service Commission, as the continued withholding of approval of new franchises was only perpetuating gridlock. Franchises for Smith Street/Clinton Street/Veeder Avenue and a new loop to serve the Alco plant were approved by the Common Council on July 17, 1911. The dispute over the widening of Nott Street was also resolved when the General Electric Schenectady Works manager G.E. Emmons, acting unofficially as a neutral arbiter, reviewed the record of the situation and concluded in a letter dated July 29, 1911 that Schenectady Railway had morally, if not legally, agreed to carry out the widening at its expense. Schenectady Railway accepted this finding and carried out the widening project the following year.

7.1 Scotia

Although work was stalled in Schenectady, the railway was still carrying out new construction in Scotia. A new branch on Ballston Avenue opened in 1905. This branch was projected to extend to the Boston and Maine railroad depot on Vley Road, but completion was delayed as Scotia sought to compel the railway to grade two new streets along the route. While not ruling officially, the P.S.C. indicated in March 1908 that it likely could not order the railway to pay this cost and urged both sides to reach an agreement. The railway completed this branch and placed it in service just before the end of 1908. In total, the branch was 0.9 miles long and followed Ballston Avenue, Wallace Street, Douglass Street (5th Street), and Vley Road to the B&M depot. Scotia trolleys began carrying "M" (Mohawk Avenue) or "B" (Ballston Avenue) placards on the front to indicate which branch they were serving.

7.2 Ballston Spa

After the D&H bought the Hudson Valley Railway Company (H.V.R.C.) in 1906, the management sought to rationalize the trackage and operations in Ballston Spa, as Schenectady Railway and H.V.R.C. were now under common ownership. Via a series of lease agreements, Schenectady Railway began using the H.V.R.C. tracks on Front Street and Milton Avenue to reach Lincoln Corner (the intersection of Milton Avenue and Malta Avenue) and abandoned its trackage on Washington Street in 1911. From Lincoln Corner, Schenectady Railway interurbans continued using the route over Mechanic Street and the D&H leased right-of-way to Saratoga, although all of this trackage was now leased to H.V.R.C.[2] Fares collected for the use of this trackage were turned over to H.V.R.C. This agreement had minimal impact for passengers, however; they paid a 40-cent fare and rode on a single car between Schenectady and Saratoga, as they did previously.

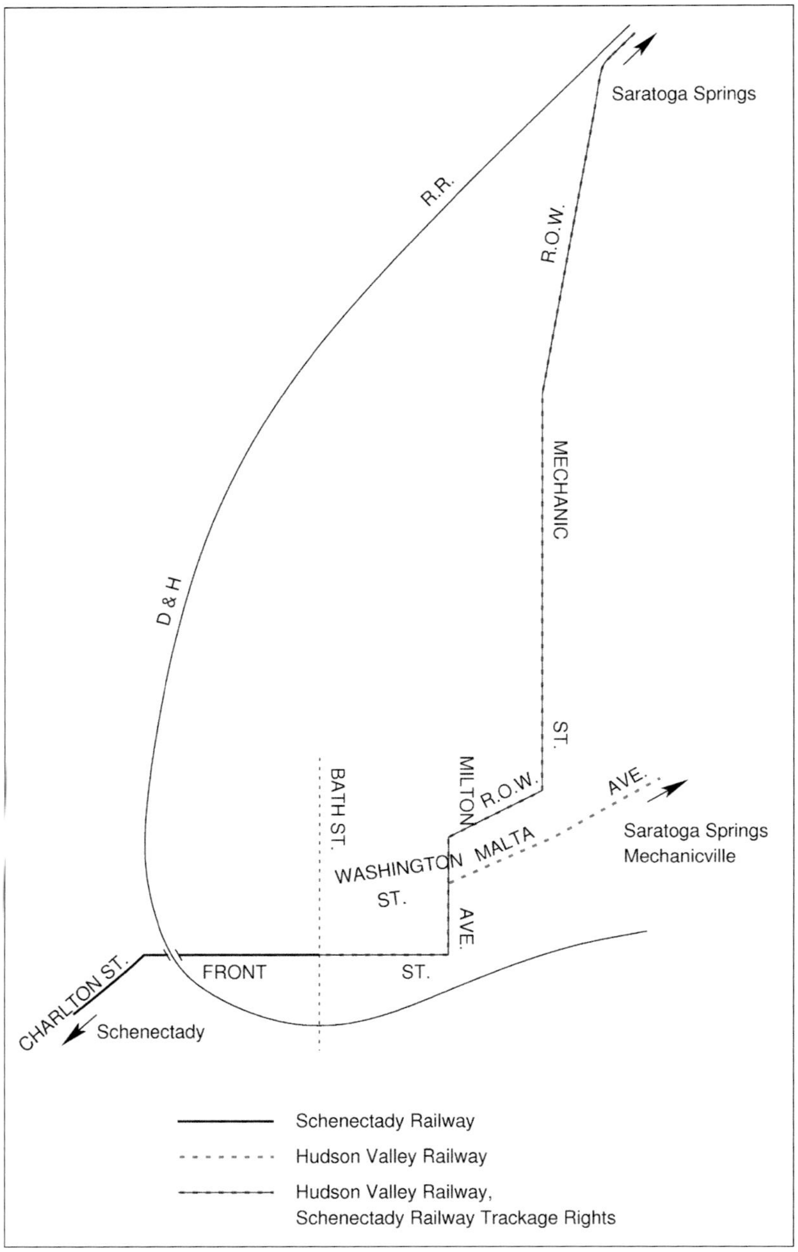

Street railway trackage in Ballston Spa, 1911. *(Map by author)*

Opposite page: A portion of the trackage on N. Jay Street serving the Alco plant, November 26, 1912, shortly after construction. Part of the Alco plant is seen on the right, while the Erie Canal is visible through the D&H railroad underpass. *(From the collection of the Efner History Center at City Hall, Schenectady)*

8

The Peak Years (1912–1922)

The P.S.C. approved the construction in downtown Schenectady later in 1911: Smith Street, from S. Center Street to Veeder Avenue (0.2 miles); Clinton Street, from Smith Street to State Street (0.1 miles); and Veeder Avenue, from Smith Street to State Street (0.1 miles).

The new trackage permitted northbound (inbound) trolleys from Bellevue to use Smith and Clinton Streets to reach State Street, while interurbans could now use Veeder Avenue to reverse direction. The trackage was in use within a year. Standing cars on Smith Street prompted complaints and a case to be taken to the P.S.C., but the situation was "settled amicably" by the parties involved, and the P.S.C. case was dismissed.

In 1912, the P.S.C. approved construction on 0.63 miles of city streets to improve access to the Alco works: Nott Street, from Park Place westward to North Jay Street; North Jay Street, from Nott Street southward to South Avenue; and South Avenue, from North Jay Street eastward to Park Place.

Approval was also given for an extension of the Campbell Avenue line to Olean Street (0.16 miles) and relocation of the trackage on Hattie Place to Nott Street (0.13 miles), while a 0.25-mile extension of the Mohawk Avenue branch in Scotia to Toll Street was completed the following year. The short segment of track on Hattie Place between Van Vranken Avenue and Nott Street was abandoned.

It would appear that the deal with the city council was reached just in time for the railway as the Socialists won control of the city council and the mayor's office in the 1911 elections. A franchise for laying a second track on part of Rugby Road was still being debated as 1911 drew to a close, and when the new aldermen took office, the Socialists made it clear that they would not approve any more franchises for Schenectady Railway until the railway resumed selling six tickets for a quarter and constructed a pedestrian walkway on the Cotton Factory Hollow bridge at its own expense. Consequently, there was no further activity of significance in street railway matters at the city council in 1912 and 1913. After a Fusion majority won control in the 1913 elections, an ordinance for the double-tracking on Rugby Road was finally approved on April 20, 1914.

With new downtown trackage finally in place, Schenectady Railway built a grand new waiting room and ticket office at 512 State Street. Opened on October 21, 1913, the building had a "T" shaped floor plan with a main entrance on State Street and a side entrance on Lafayette Street. The State Street entrance had a 45-foot-tall arched entryway and a large clock concentric with the arch. The main portion of the waiting room, which was the long part of the "T," stretched back from this entrance and had correspondingly tall ceilings. One side had a marble ticket office, a newsstand, and telephone booths while the other had seating for 125. An additional waiting area was located in the back of the building, along with the Lafayette Street entrance, restrooms, and access to the offices on the upper two floors.

Schenectady Railway waiting room. (*American Architect, Google Books*)

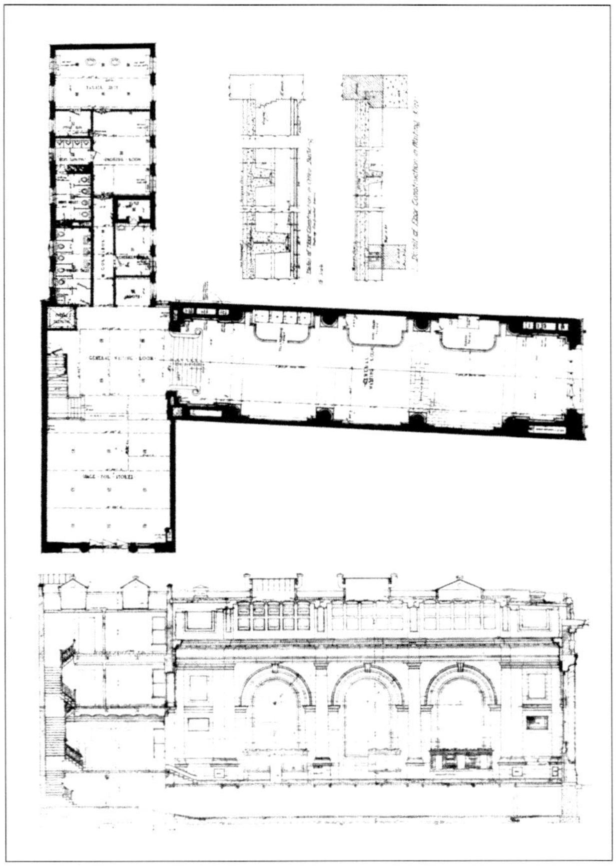

Schenectady Railway waiting room.
(*American Architect, Google Books*)

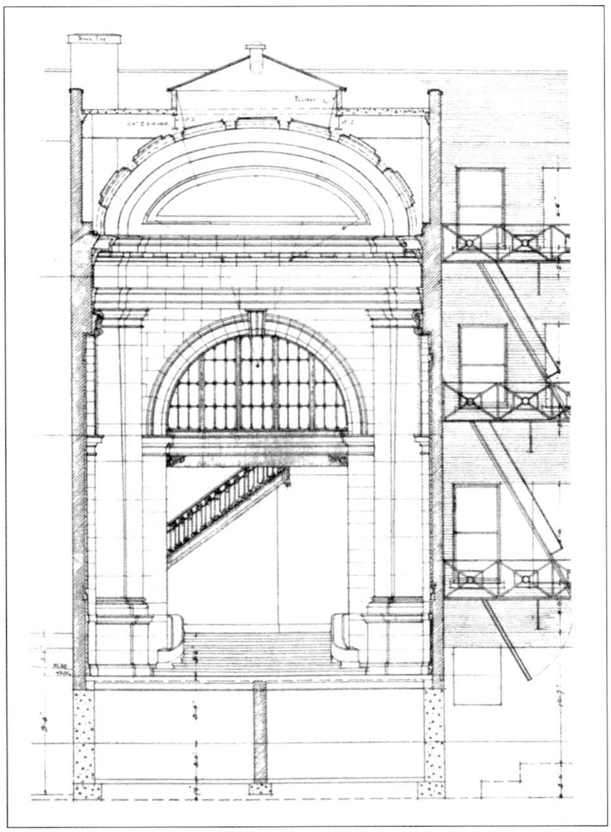

The front entrance to the Schenectady Railway waiting room at 512 State Street. (*From the collection of the Efner History Center at City Hall, Schenectady*)

In 1914, the P.S.C. again refused the city's request to compel the sale of six tickets for a quarter. In a ruling handed down on May 20, 1914, the P.S.C. concluded that the 5 cent fare was not unjust or unreasonable, noting that a street railway company should be profitable with a reasonable rate of return. The rate of return for Schenectady Railway at the time was calculated to be around 8 or 9 percent; many argued that this figure actually overestimated the ultimate return to shareholders when future capital expenditures and costs of compliance with new rules are considered.

The city expanded again in 1914 when approximately 90 acres of land along State and Albany Streets were annexed. The annexed territory was 0.4 miles in length and extended roughly 0.1 miles north of State Street and 0.1 miles south of Albany Street. The "Ivy League streets" (Harvard Street, Yale Street, etc.) make up a significant part of this area today. Much development was taking place along the Albany and Schenectady Turnpike, and the interurban railway was evidently a major driver.

In 1915, the Schenectady Railway's first new line in eight years was approved—a line to serve Grand Boulevard in Schenectady and Niskayuna. The general feeling expressed by the council was that the railway should expand its service to justify the fares being collected—quite a reversal from previous years. The line started at the corner of Van Vranken Avenue and Nott Street and followed Nott Street eastward to Grand Boulevard, which it then followed in a private median right-of-way to Van Antwerp Street. Part of this route had already been built (on Nott Street from Van Vranken Avenue to Wendell Avenue). The remainder consisted of 1.6 miles of new construction, of which 0.5 miles were located in the town of Niskayuna. This would be the last new trackage laid by the company.

The neighborhood served by this new line originated with a 1904 land purchase by W. Garner Bee. Led by Bee, the Grand Boulevard Association began developing the land into a neighborhood of upper-middle-class homes. Whereas the G.E. Plot was generally affordable only for those in the uppermost class of society, such as presidents and vice-presidents, the Grand Boulevard neighborhood was built to attract people in the next tier, such as managers and engineers, who wanted and could afford significantly better-than-average homes. The Grand Boulevard Association naturally lobbied for the extension of trolley service to the developing neighborhood. The construction of this neighborhood also started the transition of the town of Niskayuna from a sparsely populated rural community to a suburb, though later development was based on automobile transportation.

Caricature of W. Garner Bee with a representation of the Grand Boulevard housing development. Note the trolley running down the median of the boulevard. (*From the collection of the Efner History Center at City Hall, Schenectady*)

A 2018 view of houses on Grand Boulevard, which was developed as an upper-middle-class neighborhood. (*Photography by Robert Emerson*)

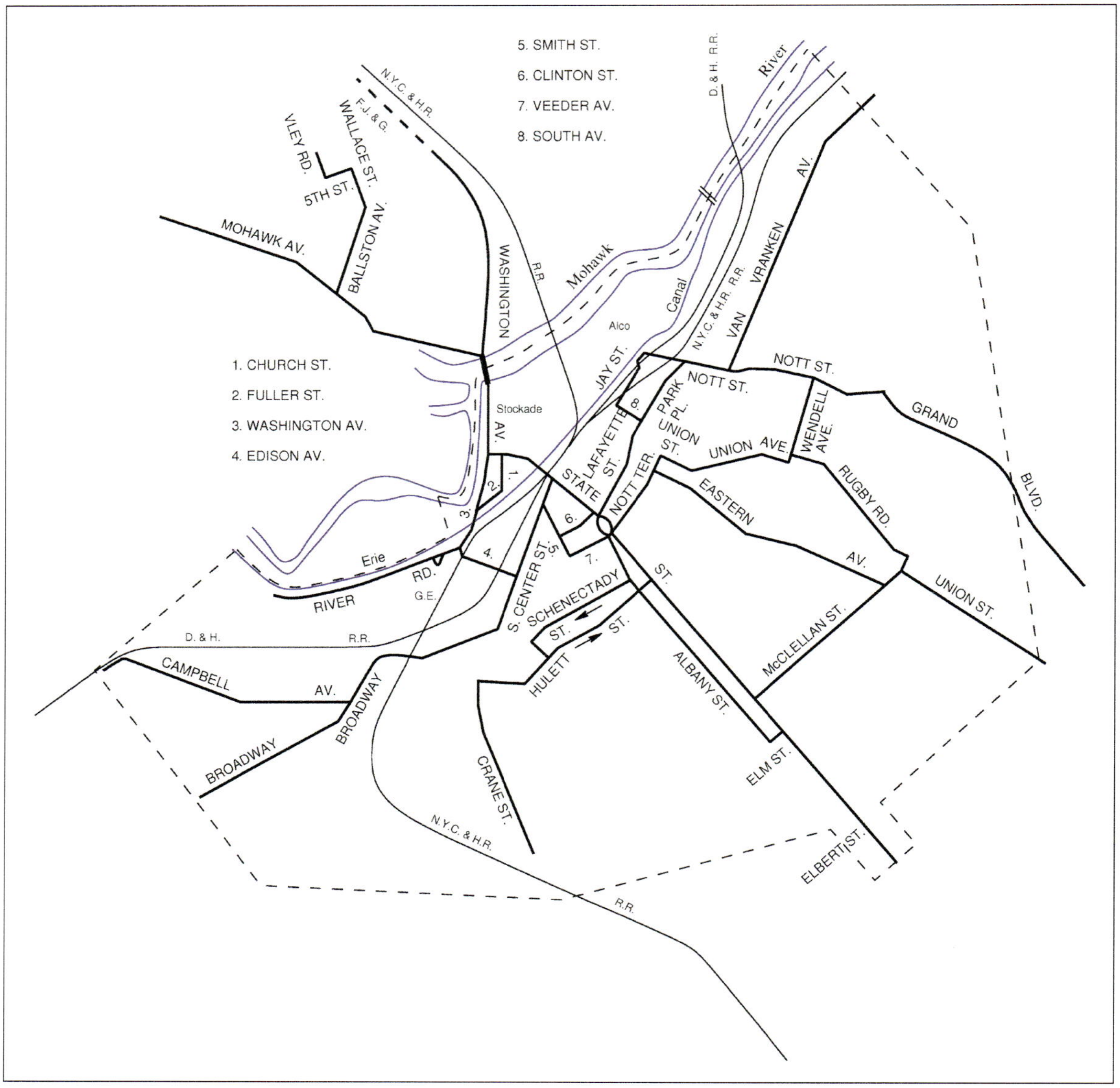

Above: Routes of Schenectady Railway in Schenectady (total length: 21.8 miles) and Scotia (total length: 2.37 miles), 1916. (*Map by author*)

Left: A 2018 view along Grand Boulevard showing examples of the houses that were built. The path between the trees on the median of Grand Blvd. looks just wide enough for a single trolley track. (*Photography by Robert Emerson*)

For years, Saratoga Springs had no depot for interurban passengers as H.V.R.C. and the city argued over laying tracks in Broadway to connect the Mechanicville and Glens Falls lines. The dispute was finally resolved in 1915, and the agreement included the construction of an interurban station worthy of a city of Saratoga's stature. H.V.R.C. opened a Beaux-Arts interurban station with a plaza in front at the corner of Broadway and Congress Street the following spring. A large waiting room was included, along with a lunch room, restrooms, offices, and a ladies lounge. Three stub-end tracks were provided for the interurbans along with three low-level platforms, each having a canopy. Schenectady Railway used this station for its Schenectady–Saratoga service as well. With this upgrade, both ends of Schenectady Railway's premier route had new, stately facilities for passengers.

Albany also received a terminal upgrade of sorts when the landmark Flemish-Gothic Delaware and Hudson building was constructed at State Street and Broadway. The plaza in front of the building was the location of a large new trolley loop that became the new terminus for the interurban runs. Connections with local United Traction cars as well as another interurban line to Hudson were available at the plaza.

The total mileage of the trolley routes serving Schenectady was now at its peak of 104.7 miles.[1] Ridership continued to trend upward through the decade. Forest Park became more of an amusement park with thrill rides by this time. Luna Park in Rexford was another place where Schenectadians could go for amusement rides.

Interurban service remained steady, with three or four trips every hour and hourly express parlor cars during the day between Schenectady and Albany. Service to Troy during the day was generally every half hour during the afternoon. Service to Saratoga during the day was generally hourly, although frequency increased during peak times such as summer Saturdays. Additional trips to Ballston Spa during the afternoon were generally included as well. The scheduled running times on the Albany (forty-five minutes express, fifty-two minutes local) and Troy (one hour and eight minutes) lines were pretty much the same as they were when service started, but the scheduled trip time from Schenectady to Saratoga (one hour and three minutes) showed some improvement.

A 2018 view of the handsome 1916 Saratoga Springs interurban terminal. (*Photography by Robert Emerson*)

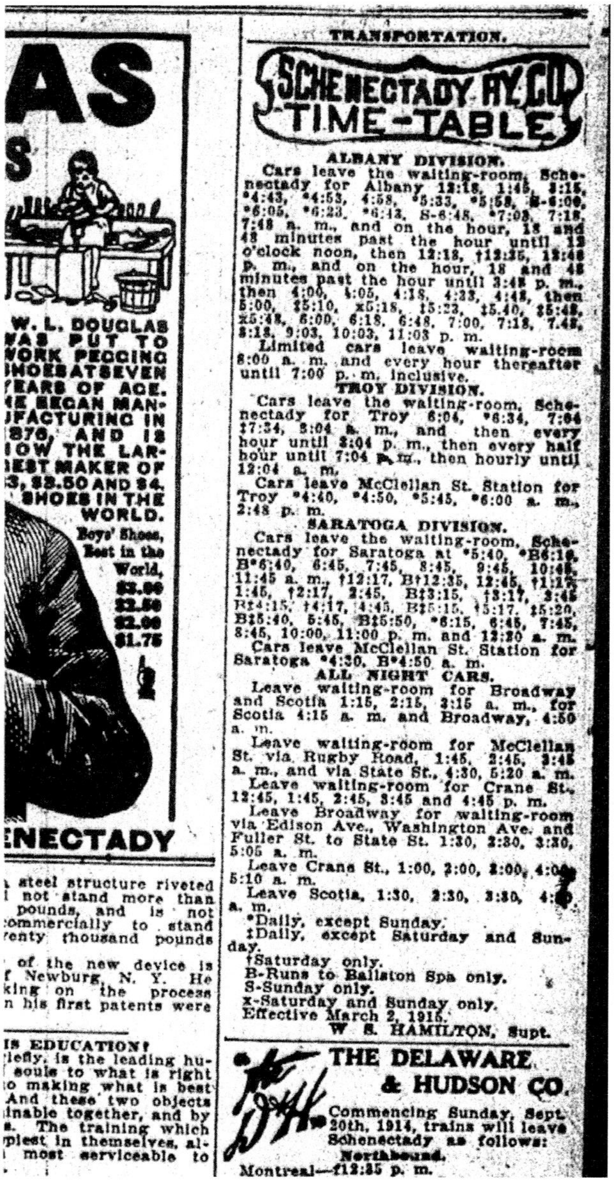

TRANSPORTATION.

SCHENECTADY RY. CO. TIME-TABLE

ALBANY DIVISION.

Cars leave the waiting-room, Schenectady for Albany 12:18, 1:45, 3:15, *4:43, *4:53, 4:58, *5:33, *5:58, S-6:00, *6:05, *6:23, *6:43, S-6:48, *7:03, 7:18, 7:48 a. m., and on the hour, 18 and 48 minutes past the hour until 12 o'clock noon, then 12:18, †12:35, 12:48 p. m., and on the hour, 18 and 48 minutes past the hour until 3:48 p. m., then 4:00, 4:05, 4:18, 4:33, 4:48, then 5:00, ‡5:10, x5:18, ‡5:23, ‡5.40, ‡5:48, x5:48, 6:00, 6:18, 6:48, 7:00, 7:18, 7.48, 8:18, 9:03, 10:03, 11:03 p. m.

Limited cars leave waiting-room 8:00 a. m. and every hour thereafter until 7:00 p. m. inclusive.

TROY DIVISION.

Cars leave the waiting-room, Schenectady for Troy 6:04, *6:34, 7:04 ‡7:34, 8:04 a. m., and then every hour until 3:04 p. m., then every half hour until 7:04 p. m., then hourly until 12:04 a. m.

Cars leave McClellan St. Station for Troy *4:40, *4:50, *5:45, *6:00 a. m., 2:48 p. m.

SARATOGA DIVISION.

Cars leave the waiting-room, Schenectady for Saratoga at *5:40, *B6:10, B*6:40, 6:45, 7:45, 8:45, 9:45, 10:45, 11:45 a. m., †12:17, B†12:35, 12:45, †1:17, 1:45, †2:17, 2:45, B‡3:15, †3:17, 3:45 B‡4:15, †4:17, 4:45, B‡5:15, †5:17, ‡5:20, B‡5:40, 5:45, B‡5:50, *6:15, 6:45, 7:45, 8:45, 10:00, 11:00 p. m. and 12:20 a. m.

Cars leave McClellan St. Station for Saratoga *4:30, B*4:50 a. m.

ALL NIGHT CARS.

Leave waiting-room for Broadway and Scotia 1:15, 2:15, 3:15 a. m., for Scotia 4:15 a. m. and Broadway, 4:50 a. m.

Leave waiting-room for McClellan St. via Rugby Road, 1:45, 2:45, 3:45 a. m., and via State St., 4:30, 5:20 a. m.

Leave waiting-room for Crane St., 12:45, 1:45, 2:45, 3:45 and 4:45 p. m.

Leave Broadway for waiting-room via Edison Ave., Washington Ave. and Fuller St. to State St. 1:30, 2:30, 3:30, 5:05 a. m.

Leave Crane St., 1:00, 2:00, 3:00, 4:00, 5:10 a. m.

Leave Scotia, 1:30, 2:30, 3:30, 4:[illegible] a. m.

*Daily, except Sunday.

‡Daily, except Saturday and Sunday.

†Saturday only.

B-Runs to Ballston Spa only.

S-Sunday only.

x-Saturday and Sunday only.

Effective March 2, 1915.

W. S. HAMILTON, Supt.

THE DELAWARE & HUDSON CO.

Commencing Sunday, Sept. 20th, 1914, trains will leave Schenectady as follows:

Northbound.

Montreal—f12:35 p. m.

Schenectady Railway interurban schedule, March 2, 1915. (*Schenectady Gazette, Schenectady County Public Library*)

The following are Schenectady Railway ridership statistics, 1907–32:

Year Ending	Number of Fares Collected	Year Ending	Number of Fares Collected
June 1907	13,640,000	Dec. 1920	24,741,890
June 1908	13,635,087	Dec. 1921	20,786,837
June 1909	12,432,272	Dec. 1922	21,200,958
June 1910	16,023,890	Dec. 1923	14,078,925
June 1911	18,316,130	Dec. 1924	20,412,655
June 1912	18,852,418	Dec. 1925	20,420,234
June 1913	20,819,641	Dec. 1926	21,267,322
June 1914	21,670,849	Dec. 1927	17,846,661
June 1915	18,953,280	Dec. 1928	16,495,945
Dec. 1916	19,801,118	Dec. 1929	15,486,290
Dec. 1917	21,235,632	Dec. 1930	12,421,970
Dec. 1918	22,176,983	Dec. 1931	8,790,295
Dec. 1919	23,728,358	Dec. 1932	6,416,611

Stop 20 (White's) on Albany interurban line, 1920. *(From the collection of the Efner History Center at City Hall, Schenectady)*

Stop 20 (White's) on Albany interurban line, 1920. *(From the collection of the Efner History Center at City Hall, Schenectady)*

Schenectady Railway no. 651 was part of a group of six cars built in 1916 by the Cincinnati Car Company. These cars were used regularly for the Saratoga service. (*From the collection of the Efner History Center at City Hall, Schenectady*)

World War I would bring new difficulties to Schenectady Railway. Although patronage continued to increase, the cost of serving those patrons would increase rapidly (approximately 15 percent per year) while revenues would remain comparatively flat because of the 5-cent fare limit. Whereas previous debates were about lowering the fare, Schenectady Railway now found it necessary to request a fare increase. The company cut its dividend nearly in half in 1917 and stopped paying any dividend afterward. Since the 5-cent fare was fixed in every railway franchise since the initial one in 1886, council approval would be needed for a fare increase, at least for trips within the city.

Given the previous acrimony, one can easily imagine how popular that would be, and politically, the aldermen would have difficulty approving an increase whether or not they recognized the new financial difficulties caused by the war. Desire to support the wages of railway workers finally become sufficient to push through a temporary (one-year) increase to 6 cents in 1919 and another temporary increase to 7 cents in 1920. Since wage increases provided by the company offset the additional revenue, the company remained in financial difficulty. The authorization for the 7-cent fare within the city was set to expire on May 31, 1921, but an amendment to the state public service law in March gave the Public Service Commission supremacy over any local ordinances or franchise requirements; the 7-cent fare hence remained in effect indefinitely.

Ridership reached an all-time high in 1920 with 24.7 million fare-paying passengers. The drop in ridership for 1921 was not surprising given the steep post-war depression. However, the subsequent recovery in other economic sectors would not be seen in the street railway industry.

GDP price deflator, showing the price level by year and the scale of inflation arising during World War I. (*Chart by author*)

Evening rush hour at the G.E. loop, c. 1917. (*From the collection of the Efner History Center at City Hall, Schenectady*)

Any obstruction to traffic could quickly result in a lengthy back-up. This scene is on State Street, looking west from the railroad overpass. (*From the collection of the Efner History Center at City Hall, Schenectady*)

* * * * *

A view of State Street on June 6, 1923, during the strike, when trolleys began to be stoned by crowds. (*From the collection of the Efner History Center at City Hall, Schenectady*)

9

Decline (1923–1929)

The years following World War I would not be any easier for the street railways. With prices falling (though not to pre-war levels), Schenectady Railway sought to cut wages back as part of an effort to regain profitability and financial stability. Naturally, such moves were not popular. Tensions were heightened by the unwillingness of the railway management, especially the new general manager, Harry Weatherwax, to recognize the employees' union. Weatherwax came from the D&H, which had long had a policy of not recognizing unions. In the past, Schenectady Railway had not recognized unions either, but the input of union leaders was nevertheless received and considered by management. Strikes in the past had been fairly few and short-lived, and the city's residents, who depended on the streetcars to get to their own jobs, were generally not very supportive of the strikers.

The Amalgamated Association of Street and Electric Railway Employees of America, Division 576, voted to strike on May 16, 1923, when the railway cut wages by 25 percent and Weatherwax refused to recognize or negotiate with the union. This strike would become bitter and violent. Patronage plummeted immediately as the sympathy of a clear majority of city residents was with the strikers. Things turned violent on June 6 when trolleys operated by strikebreakers were stoned and attacked by mobs. Jitneys were organized throughout the community to provide alternative transportation for streetcar patrons. In August, Schenectady Railway offered "special compensation" to strikers who returned to work by the end of the month. Eventually, most workers were hired back, and matters gradually returned to normal. Workers soon received a pay raise, though the company officially still did not recognize the union. Both the workers and the company were in fact facing the same problem—a long-term decline in revenue.

Twenty-two new cars were purchased from Brill in the mid-1920s for city service. These cars would be the last purchased by Schenectady Railway.

The city of Schenectady was still expanding. The Woodlawn neighborhood was annexed in 1923, thus moving the city boundary another 1.2 miles out State Street to the southeast. In addition to the Albany interurbans, Schenectady Railway designated a Woodlawn route that ran out State Street as far as Stop 6 near the new city line.

Patronage, though still fairly high, gradually dropped as the 1920s progressed. The reason is quite apparent; automobile ownership was soaring. Automobile ownership also cut into park attendance significantly, and hence Schenectady Railway sold its parks. Brandywine Park was sold in the middle of the decade, and Forest Park was subdivided into lots shortly afterward.

The company's financial situation, which was already quite poor at the start of the decade, deteriorated further. Fares were increased to 10 cents in 1928. Other electric railroads were in worse shape: Hudson Valley Railway ceased all operations at the end of 1928. Schenectady Railway purchased the Saratoga Springs station from H.V.R.C. and continued operation of its Saratoga line.

The fare increase was insufficient to avoid bankruptcy, however; Schenectady Railway entered receivership in 1929. The company's difficult financial condition was quite pronounced, even during the generally prosperous decade of the Roaring Twenties.

10

End of Rail Service

(1930–1946)

The Great Depression would precipitate major changes to the Schenectady Railway and its network. In 1930, before the severity of the Depression had taken hold, Schenectady Railway made some significant changes to its routes in the northeastern part of the city. The McClellan Street route (State Street eastward to McClellan Street to Union Street) was restored, while a new Eastern Avenue route from State Street eastward over Nott Terrace and Eastern Avenue to the intersection of Union and McClellan Streets was established. The Union Avenue and Grand Boulevard routes were combined into a single new Grand Boulevard route by rerouting Grand Boulevard cars over the previous Union Avenue route instead of Lafayette and Nott Streets. The "A" Belt and "B" Belt routes were eliminated as part of this change, as was the Union Avenue route (save for a couple of daily shoppers' specials that operated over Lafayette and Nott Streets to Wendell Avenue). Once again, however, the Belt routes were restored shortly afterward.

In an effort to maintain patronage, the FJ&G in 1931 invested in five streamlined Brill cars. Numbered 125 to 129, these cars, along with eleven similar third rail-powered vehicles built for the Philadelphia and Western, would become known as the "Bullet" cars.[1] A wind tunnel was used to design them. Capable of 92 mph, these cars were intended to attract riders with higher speeds and a modern look.[2] No other Bullet cars were manufactured; these sixteen constituted the total production.

The faster speeds enabled the FJ&G to reduce the scheduled travel time to an hour from Gloversville to Schenectady. These cars helped sustain ridership for a time, but the financial problems continued; FJ&G was also losing money on its electric passenger service.

Around this time, street railway companies across the country were deciding that rubber-tired buses had become preferable vehicles for providing public transportation, citing the flexibility of operating on any paved street and maneuvering around obstacles. In Schenectady, as in most other American cities, the city's residents were paying for paving the streets virtually everywhere that street railways did not operate. Schenectady Railway thus began substituting buses for trolleys on the company's routes. Bus conversions took place on the following dates:

Crane Street—June 16, 1930
Scotia—April 2, 1931
Eastern Avenue—October 10, 1933
Woodlawn—April 1, 1934
Broadway—April 26, 1934
Campbell Avenue—April 26, 1934
Rugby Road—August 3, 1935
Grand Boulevard—August 3, 1935
Upper Union—August 22, 1935

Bullet car no. 127 at Crescent Park in downtown Schenectady. The waiting room is visible on the other side of State Street. *(From the collection of the Efner History Center at City Hall, Schenectady)*

Schenectady Railway also started a new bus route at this time: Rosa Road on June 16, 1930.

As the Depression deepened, the increasing financial losses and lack of sufficient patronage took their toll. The interurban runs to Albany and Troy were abandoned on July 30, 1933, and July 15, 1934, respectively.

In the mid-1930s, numbers were assigned to the local Schenectady routes:

1. Rosa Road
2. Crane Street/Scotia
3. Upper Union—Eastern Avenue to Stop 10
4. State Street to Frank Street (also Woodlawn Bus)
5. Broadway
6. State Street to McClellan Street
7. Grand Boulevard
8. Campbell Avenue
9. Rugby Road
10. Alplaus—Rexford (also Round Lake Bus)

The April 5, 1938 condemnation of the Mohawk River bridge at Washington Avenue, which was only used by trolleys at this time, brought an end to the service by the Brill Bullets as they were single-end cars and, lacking access to the loop around Crescent Park, could no longer be turned in Schenectady. The five Bullet cars were sold to the Bamberger Railroad in Utah. FJ&G electric cars now terminated in Scotia at the north side of the bridge with shuttle buses to reach Schenectady, and FJ&G brought back the 1903 St. Louis cars to maintain service. The line was completely abandoned by FJ&G shortly afterward, with the last run departing downtown Gloversville on June 28, 1938, at 10.30 p.m. and returning three and a half hours later.

The Saratoga route finally succumbed on December 6, 1941. The last run was made by car 650, which departed from the corner of Nott Street and Park Place at 11.47 p.m. The streetcar tracks had already been cut south of that point due to street construction on Nott Street; buses were then used to shuttle passengers to and from State Street. The car reached Saratoga at 12.44 a.m. Shortly afterward, the car began its return trip to Schenectady, arriving in the city at 2.13 a.m. Both the car and many structures on the line were damaged by zealous souvenir hunters. Twelve hours and eight minutes later, news from Hawaii focused people's attention on international affairs.

Due to the rationing of gasoline and rubber tires, rail service on two lines in the city of Schenectady continued through the World War II years: routes 4 and 6. By this time, trackage on South Washington Avenue had been taken up, resulting in single track operation over Church and Fuller Streets. Signals at each end of this section directed the movements of the streetcars. These two remaining lines were converted to buses on January 16, 1946, bring the era of urban rail streetcar service in Schenectady to an end.

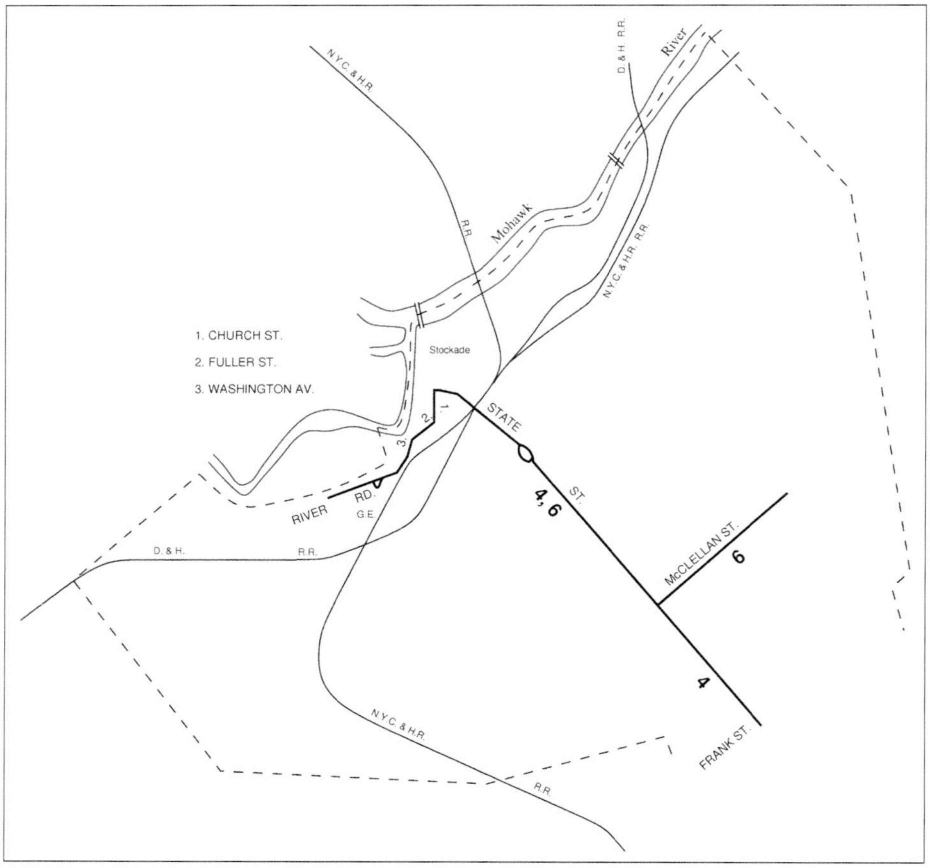

Routes of Schenectady Railway in Schenectady (total length: 4.5 miles), 1942. (*Map by author*)

Dismantling the ticket booth in the waiting room, c. 1948. (*From the collection of the Efner History Center at City Hall, Schenectady*)

11

Epilogue:
Legacy of the Trolleys

At first glance, there is little, if any, evidence today to indicate that trolleys once regularly carried passengers on the streets of Schenectady. The overhead wire and its supporting structure were removed long ago, and tracks are no longer seen in the streets—though much trackage in the city of Schenectady is apparently still in place, buried (mostly) beneath the asphalt of the city's streets. The strip of land where interurbans once traveled to Albany and Troy is now occupied by the eastbound lanes of New York State routes 5 and 7 respectively.

However, some vestiges of the trolley operations can be seen if one knows where to look. Part of the right-of-way of the Saratoga line is now a walking/biking trail, and much of the remainder is still visible as a dirt path. Piers for the trolley bridge over the Mohawk River are still in place. Some cuts, embankments, and gaps in the trees still indicate the location of the FJ&G electric railroad to Gloversville. The Saratoga Springs depot still stands, now serving as a visitor information center, and a recent renovation of 512 State Street has once again placed the name "Schenectady Railway" proudly over downtown Schenectady along with the 45-foot-tall arch of the former waiting room's façade. The brick substations for the Albany and Troy interurban lines still stand, now housing businesses instead of rotary converters.

Although most trolleys were scrapped, some were sold to other cities, and a few were later preserved by museums. The Brill Bullets in particular carried passengers for the Bamberger Railroad in and out of Salt Lake City, Utah until operations ceased in 1952. Bullet no. 127 was eventually acquired by the Orange Empire Railway Museum.

Perhaps the biggest monument to the trolleys are the cities and neighborhoods they helped construct and connect. Although their residents and workers principally use automobiles and buses for transportation now, their architecture indicates their development during a time when the trolleys were the kings of urban transit.

Looking west on the Albany line toward Stop 20, *c.* 1920. (*From the collection of the Efner History Center at City Hall, Schenectady*)

Looking west toward the location of Stop 20, 2018. (*Photo by author*)

This 2018 view looking west on Broadway in the Bellevue neighborhood shows the mixed residential and commercial development that is typical of the streets on which the trolleys ran. (*Photography by Robert Emerson*)

Above left: Looking north on Lower Broadway toward the former D&H grade crossing, 2018. The cracks suggest that there are still tracks under the asphalt. (*Photography by Robert Emerson*)

Top right: This 2018 view of Broadway shows that old streetcar rails are still in place in some of the streets of Schenectady. (*Photography by Robert Emerson*)

Above right: Another 2018 view of Broadway showing old streetcar rails. (*Photography by Robert Emerson*)

A 2018 view of the former Schenectady Railway waiting room at 512 State Street, following a recent renovation and restoration of the tall arched façade. (*Photography by Robert Emerson*)

A 2018 view of the Lafayette Street entrance of the former Schenectady Railway waiting room. (*Photography by Robert Emerson*)

A 2018 view of the former rotary converter substation at Karner's on the Albany line. (*Photography by Robert Emerson*)

A 2018 view of the former rotary converter substation at Latham's on the Troy line. (*Photography by Robert Emerson*)

Appendix I

Street Railway Franchise of 1886

WHEREAS, The Schenectady Street Railway Company, by Charles D Haines, President, did, in pursuance of chapter 252 of the laws of 1884, make application to the Common Council of the city of Schenectady, at a special meeting regularly held Feb. 25, 1886, for the right for said corporation to build, equip, maintain and operate a street railway in, through and upon the following public streets, viz: Beginning at Mohawk river bridge, thence along Washington avenue to State street, thence along State street to Brandywine avenue, thence along Brandywine avenue to Union street, thence along Union street to Centre street, through Centre street to State street; also Union street, from Washington avenue to Church street, and Church street, from Union street to State street.

WHEREAS, All the requirements of law, upon which the Common Council of the city of Schenectady may take action upon and grant such application, have been complied with; therefore, be it

Resolved, That the Common Council of the city of Schenectady hereby grants and permits its consent to the Schenectady Street Railway Company to build, equip, maintain and operate with a single track through, upon and along the following streets and avenues in said city, viz: Beginning at Mohawk river bridge, thence along Washington avenue to State street, thence along State street to Brandywine avenue, thence along Brandywine avenue to Union street, thence along Union street to Centre street, through Centre street to State street. Upon the following terms and conditions, the non-compliance with any one or more of which by said Schenectady Street Railway Company shall work a forfeiture of the grant and permission, viz:

First—The operation of said railway shall be subject to all the provisions of the laws of the State of New York pertaining to street railways and the amendments thereof.

Second—The work is to be done under the supervision of the City Surveyor and the Committee on Roads and Bridges of the Common Council, as to seeing that the streets are left, on completion of the road, in as good condition as found; to see that the company conforms to the grade of the streets and not to interfere with the water, sewer or gas pipes, or any of the appliances or attachments used in connection with either of the same; that there be no turnouts on Centre street; that the guage [*sic.*] of the road shall be not less than 3 feet 6 inches between the tracks.

Third—The rail to be used shall be of the style known as "T" rail, and when laid shall be flush with the surface of the street. All the work shall be done in a workmanlike manner.

Fourth—The rate of fare shall not exceed five cents for each passenger for one continuous ride over the whole or any part of said road.

Fifth—Said street railway company shall, whenever as required and under the supervision of the Common Council of the city of Schenectady, keep in permanent repair that portion of every street between its tracks, the rails of its tracks, and a space two feet in width outside of and adjoining the outside rails of its tracks, as long as it shall continue to use such tracks, so constructed as foresaid, at its own cost and expense.

Sixth—No other than animal or horse power shall be used by said company in the operation of its said road.

Seventh—The Common Council reserves the right to itself, and to the citizens of Schenectady, and to the Board of Water Commissioners, to construct and repair sewers and drains, or lay or repair water pipes or sewer pipes, and to connect the same with buildings on either side, on either of said streets, or to make any other excavations therein or change the grade of any of said streets, and neither the city of Schenectady, said citizens, or any of them and said Board of Water Commissioners shall be liable to said Schenectady Street Railway Company for any delay or hindrance in the operation of its said railway by reason thereof, and whenever said Common Council or said Board of Water Commissioners shall deem it proper to construct or repair a sewer or drain, or lay or repair a water pipe or sewer pipe, or make any other excavation under the track or tracks of said railway, said railway company shall take up and temporarily remove its track or tracks, and appurtenances thereto, from the place or places where said sewer, drain or water pipes, or other necessary excavations are to be made, until the work shall be done, with the privilege of temporarily laying the same along the side of such place or places.

Eighth—Said railway shall consist of a single track throughout the whole of the said route with suitable switches, sidings, turnouts, turntables and stands as may be required for the proper operation thereof.

Ninth—The said railway shall be equipped with suitable and commodious cars for the transportation of passengers, which shall make trips every day of the year, except when prevented by snow, ice or fire, not less often than once an hour, between 6:30 o'clock A.M. and 9 o'clock P.M. on week days, and when prevented from running cars by reason of ice, snow or fire, said company shall run comfortable and commodious sleighs instead of cars, at their option, when prevented from running their cars by snow.

Tenth—The city of Schenectady grants permission to said railway company to cross the railroad tracks laid upon State street.

Eleventh—The construction of said railway shall be commenced by July 1st, 1886, and completed by Nov. 1st, 1886.

Appendix II

A Short History of the FJ&G Interurban

A summary of the development of the interurban route from Gloversville to Schenectady is presented here. A much fuller history of the Fonda, Johnstown, and Gloversville electric division can be found in the references listed in the bibliography.

B.1 Gloversville/Johnstown

The first street railway in the Glove Cities was the Johnstown, Gloversville and Kingsboro, which opened a horsecar line in 1874 on Main and Perry Streets in Johnstown and Main Street in Gloversville. In 1893, the Cayadutta Electric Railroad began construction of an electric-powered railroad from Gloversville to Fonda. The Gloversville terminal was located south of downtown, near the FJ&G steam railroad grade crossing of Main Street. As the company had no street franchise in Johnstown, the Cayadutta built its line on a private right-of-way bypassing downtown. Soon afterward, the Cayadutta obtained control of both the JG&K and the FJ&G steam railroad, which was built to connect its namesake cities in 1870 and extended to Northville in 1875. The new owners kept the FJ&G name for the combined entity, leasing the other companies to it. With this combination, the JG&K was electrified and integrated with the Gloversville–Fonda trackage to form the electric division of the FJ&G. Using the street franchise of the JG&K, new trackage was built to reroute the Gloversville–Fonda line through downtown Johnstown. The bypass around Johnstown would remain in service as the "back" track.

B.2 Amsterdam

The oldest portion of the FJ&G electric division trackage was opened by the Amsterdam Street Railway in 1873. From downtown Amsterdam, this company built and operated a 1.6-mile horsecar line on Main Street that ran west to Market Street, then north on Market Street to Division Street, and then west on Division Street to Henrietta Street. In 1891, new management electrified the line and extended it west to Akin (now Fort Johnson) on private right-of-way paralleling the New York Central mainline. Another electric line up the steep grade on Market Street (14 percent—the steepest street railway grade in the state) to Harrower's opened the same year; this line was extended to Hagaman in 1902.

B.3 Linking the Mohawk Valley

The FJ&G purchased control of the Amsterdam Street Railway in 1901 and began construction of a high-speed double track overhead electric trolley line connecting it to Johnstown the following year. The new interurban line extended west from Akin and connected to the Johnstown–Fonda track at Sulphur Springs Junction just south of Johnstown. Additional trackage to permit the interurban cars to bypass local traffic was laid alongside the FJ&G steam railroad in Johnstown and Gloversville and also along West Main Street in Amsterdam. The double-track interurban route was subsequently extended eastward to Schenectady on a private right-of-way from East Main Street to a connection with Schenectady Railway trackage in Scotia. The entire route from Gloversville to Schenectady opened for service on July 1, 1903.

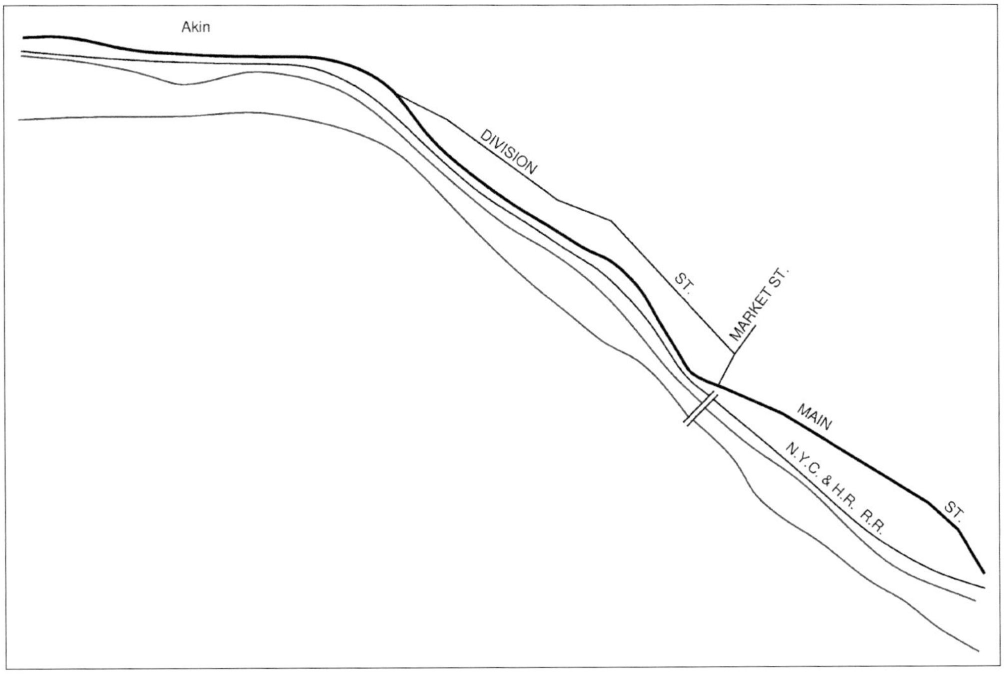

FJ&G interurban route through Amsterdam, 1903–38. (*Map by author*)

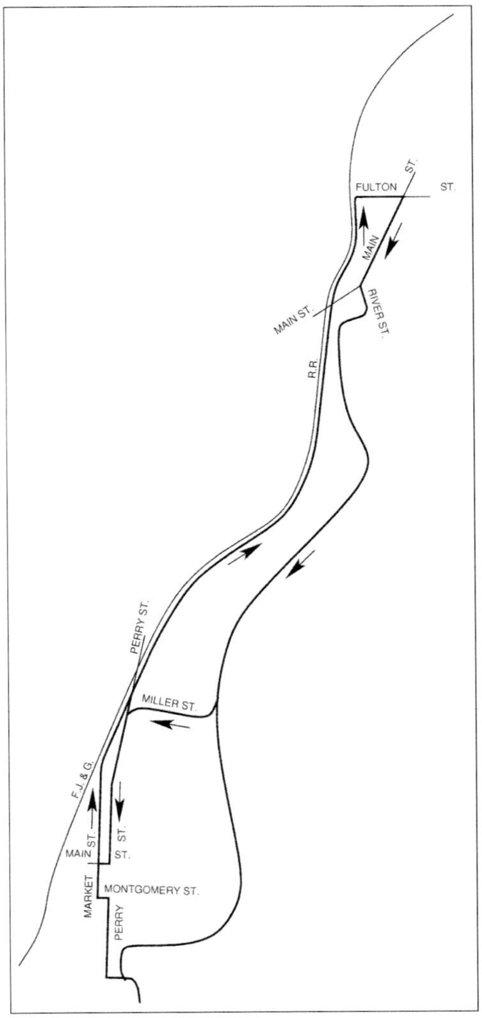

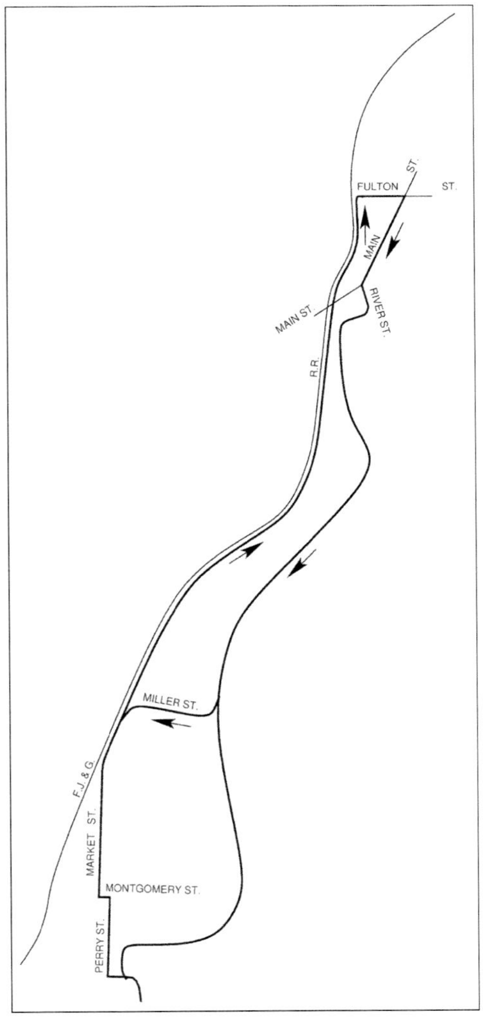

Near right: FJ&G interurban route through Johnstown and Gloversville, 1903–30. (*Map by author*)

Far right: FJ&G interurban route through Johnstown and Gloversville, 1930–38. (*Map by author*)

Appendix III

Schenectady Railway Car Roster

Schenectady Railway acquired a variety of cars over the years for transporting passengers. Unfortunately, the available records of passenger equipment in the early years of the company are incomplete. During those years, most street railway companies numbered their cars sequentially as they were acquired or placed in service. Around 1903, Schenectady Railway began reassigning three-digit numbers to each car, with the first digit indicating the type or class of car.

The list here is compiled from various sources. Conflicts are resolved by the author's judgment of which data is most consistent with other available information. A few educated guesses, indicated by question marks (?), are included.

Schenectady Street Railway Company

Car Numbers	Builder	Year	Length	Motors	Notes
1–5	Stephenson	1886			Horsecars; converted to electric 1891
6–11	Gilbert	1891	28'	Edison No. 12 (2 × 25 hp)	
12–17	Jones	1893	26'		8 bench

Schenectady Railway Company

Car Numbers	Builder	Year	Length	Motors	Previous Numbers	Notes
3–71			Renumbered 1903 – see below			
100s: Single truck closed cars						
100–102	Brill		26'	GE-67* (2 × 40 hp)	3–5	Second cars w/nos. 3–5?
103–108	Gilbert	1891	28'	GE-67* (2 × 40 hp)	6–11	10→108
109–128	Stephenson	1900	28'	GE-67 (2 × 40 hp)	22–41	
129–136	St. Louis	1901	30'	GE-57 (2 × 50 hp)	42–49	
137–142	Brill	1904	31'	GE-80 (2 × 40 hp)		
200s: Double truck closed cars						
200–203	St. Louis	1899		GE-52 (4 × 25 hp)	18–21	
200–221	Brill	1924–25	40'			

Car Numbers	Builder	Year	Length	Motors	Previous Numbers	Notes
300s: Single truck open cars						
300–305	Jones	1893	26'	GE-67* (2 × 40 hp)	12–17	8 bench
306–331	Jones	1903–05	27'	GE-67 (2 × 40 hp)		9 bench
400s: Double truck open cars						
400–411	Laconia	1902	39'	GE-67 (4 × 40 hp)		13 bench
500s: Double truck interurban cars, 40'–48'						
500–511	St. Louis	1902	40'	GE-57 (4 × 50 hp)	60–71	
512–517	St. Louis	1907	41'	GE-57 (4 × 50 hp)		
518–523	St. Louis	1907	42'	GE-87 (4 × 60 hp)		
525	Laconia	1902	45'	GE-80 (4 × 40 hp)		Rebuilt from 404
550–555	St. Louis	1901	48'	GE-73 (4 × 75 hp)	50–55	
556–559	Stephenson	1902	46'	GE-73 (4 × 75 hp)	56–59	
560–564	Wason	1907	52'	GE-57 (4 × 50 hp)		Purchased from Albany Southern 1914
600s: Double truck interurban cars, 50'						
600–605	Brill	1902	51'	GE-73 (4 × 75 hp)		
606–611	Jones	1904	51'	GE-66 (4 × 125 hp)		
612	Jones	1904	51'	GE-66 (4 × 125 hp)		Rebuilt from 611
650–655	Cincinnati	1916	50'	?		
700s: Double truck closed cars						
712–723	Kuhlman	1905	44'	GE-74 (4 × 65 hp)		
800s: Double truck closed cars						
800–817	St. Louis	1912–13	42'	GE-203A (4 × 50 hp)		
850–859	Cincinnati	1917	50'	GE-258A (4 × 25 hp)		Peter Witt type

*: Installed at time of renumbering

Appendix IV

Schenectady City Route Designations

Below is a list of route designations that were used on trolleys operating in the city. For each designation, a list of streets is provided indicating the route followed by the streetcars bearing that designation. Although variations of the routes shown here may have been used at times, the routes specified below were generally used for the period of time indicated. The years of operation are the best estimates available. The routes listed here are drawn from a number of sources.

"A" Belt

(1902–1906) From G.E. Works: River Rd., Washington Ave., Fuller St., Church St., State St., Nott Terrace, Union St., Union Ave., Union Ave. East (Rugby Rd.), McClellan St., and State St. back to Washington Ave., River Rd., and G.E. Works.

(1906–1933) From G.E. Works: River Rd., Washington Ave., Fuller St., Church St., State St., Nott Terrace, Eastern Ave., McClellan St., and State St. back to Washington Ave., River Rd., and G.E. Works.

"B" Belt

(1902–1906) From G.E. Works: River Rd., Washington Ave., Fuller St., Church St., State St., McClellan St., Union Ave. East (Rugby Rd.), Union Ave., Union St., Nott Terrace, and State St. back to Washington Ave., River Rd., and G.E. Works.

(1906–1933) From G.E. Works: River Rd., Washington Ave., Fuller St., Church St., State St., McClellan St., Eastern Ave., Nott Terrace, and State St. back to Washington Ave., River Rd., and G.E. Works.

Albany Street

(1901–1931) Outbound: Albany St., Elm St., and State St. to Elbert St.
Return: State St. to downtown

Aqueduct

(1902–1941) Outbound: Lafayette St., Park Place, Nott St., Van Vranken Ave., and right-of-way to Aqueduct
Return: same route

Bellevue

(1901–1902) same as Campbell Avenue

(1902–1934) same as Broadway

Broadway

(1902–1934) Outbound: S. Center St. (Broadway), Broadway to Olean St.
Return: same route

Campbell Avenue

(1901–1912) Outbound: S. Center St. (Broadway), Broadway, and Campbell Ave. to 16th St.
Return: same route

(1912–1934) Outbound: S. Center St. (Broadway), Broadway, and Campbell Ave. to Olean St.
Return: same route

Crane Street

(1905–1930) same as Mont Pleasant

Eastern Avenue

(1930–1933) Outbound: State St., Nott Terrace, Eastern Ave., and McClellan St. to Union St.
Return: same route

G.E. Loop

(1899–1946) same as G.E. Works

G.E. Terminal

(1899–1946) Outbound: State St., Washington Ave., and River Rd. approximately 3,500 feet to G.E. Terminal
Return: River Rd., Washington Ave., Fuller St., Church St., and State St.
Note: 1910–1946, some trips took State St., S. Center St. (Broadway), and Edison Ave. to River Rd. and returned same route

G.E. Works

(1899–1946) Outbound: State St., Washington Ave., and River Rd. to loop at G.E. Works
Return: River Rd., Washington Ave., Fuller St., Church St., and State St.
Note: 1910-1946, some trips took State St., S. Center St. (Broadway), and Edison Ave. to River Rd. and returned same route

Grand Boulevard

(1915–1930) Outbound: Lafayette St., Park Place, Nott St., and Grand Blvd. to Van Antwerp St.
Return: same route

(1930–1935) Outbound: State St., Nott Terrace, Union St., Union Ave., Wendell Ave., Nott St., and Grand Blvd. to Van Antwerp St.
Return: same route

McClellan Street

(1904–1946) Outbound: State St., McClellan St. to car barn
Return: same route

Mont Pleasant

(1905–1930) Outbound: Albany St., Schenectady St., Strong Ave., Hulett St., Francis Ave., and Crane St. to Pearl St.
Return: Crane St., Francis Ave., Hulett St., and State St.

Rosendale Road

(1904–1935) Outbound: Nott Terrace, Union St., Union Ave., Union Ave. East (Rugby Rd.), McClellan St., and Union St. to Rosendale Rd.
Return: same route
Note: 1905–1906, route operated as shuttle on Union St. between McClellan St. and Rosendale Rd.

Rexford

(1904–1941) Outbound: Lafayette St., Park Place, Nott St., Van Vranken Ave., and right-of-way to Rexford
Return: same route
Note: some trips operated via Nott Terrace, Union St., Union Ave., Wendell Ave., Nott St., and Hattie Place to and from Van Vranken Ave.

Scotia

(1902–1905) Outbound: State St., Washington Ave., Mohawk Bridge, dyke, and Mohawk Ave. to Eagle St.
Return: same route

Scotia "B"

(1905–1908) Outbound: State St., Washington Ave., Mohawk Bridge, dyke, Mohawk Ave., and Ballston Ave. to Wallace St.
Return: same route

(1908–1931) Outbound: State St., Washington Ave., Mohawk Bridge, dyke, Mohawk Ave., Ballston Ave., Wallace St., Douglass St. (5th St.), and Vley Rd. to B&M depot
Return: same route

Scotia "M"

(1905–1912) Outbound: State St., Washington Ave., Mohawk Bridge, dyke, and Mohawk Ave. to Eagle St.
Return: same route

(1912–1931) Outbound: State St., Washington Ave., Mohawk Bridge, dyke, and Mohawk Ave. to Toll St.
Return: same route

State Street

(1901–1946) Outbound: State St. to Elbert St.
Return: same route

Union Avenue

(1899–1930) Outbound: Nott Terrace, Union St., Union Ave., and Wendell Ave. to Nott St.
Return: same route

Van Vranken Avenue

(1902–1941) Outbound: Lafayette St., Park Place, Nott St., and Van Vranken Ave. to Wood Ave.
Return: same route

Woodlawn

(1923–1934) Outbound: State St. to Stop 6
Return: same route

Appendix V

Map of Schenectady Railway, *c.* 1907

The map shown on the following four pages is an enlargement of the map found in the middle of a brochure titled *Trolley Trips* published by Schenectady Railway. The brochure is undated, but the presence of the complete line to Saratoga Springs and the absence of the extension to the B&M depot in Scotia date the map to the latter half of 1907 or 1908. Beside having a map, the brochure provided a description of points of interest throughout the territory served by the electric railroads in the Capital District.

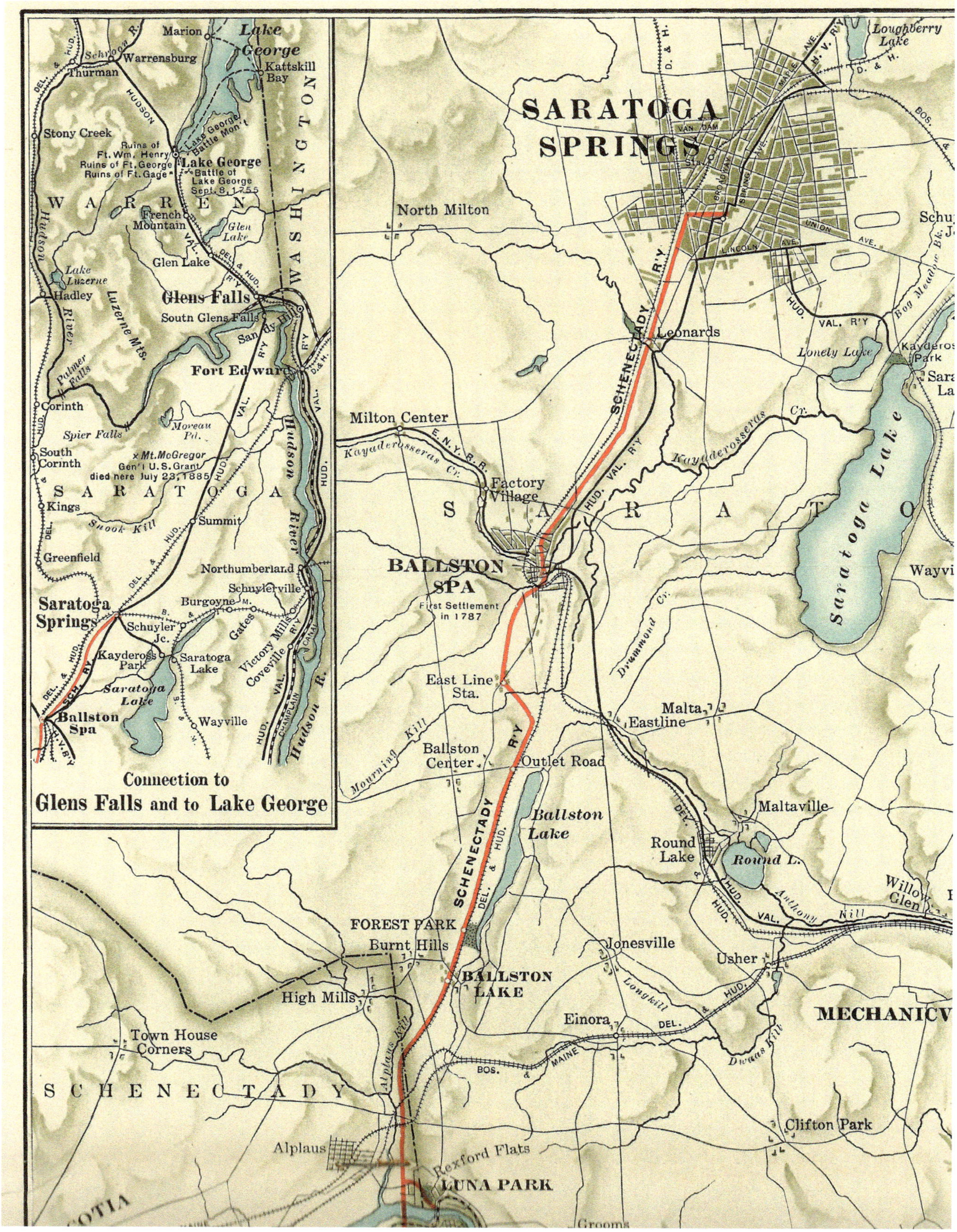

(Author's collection)

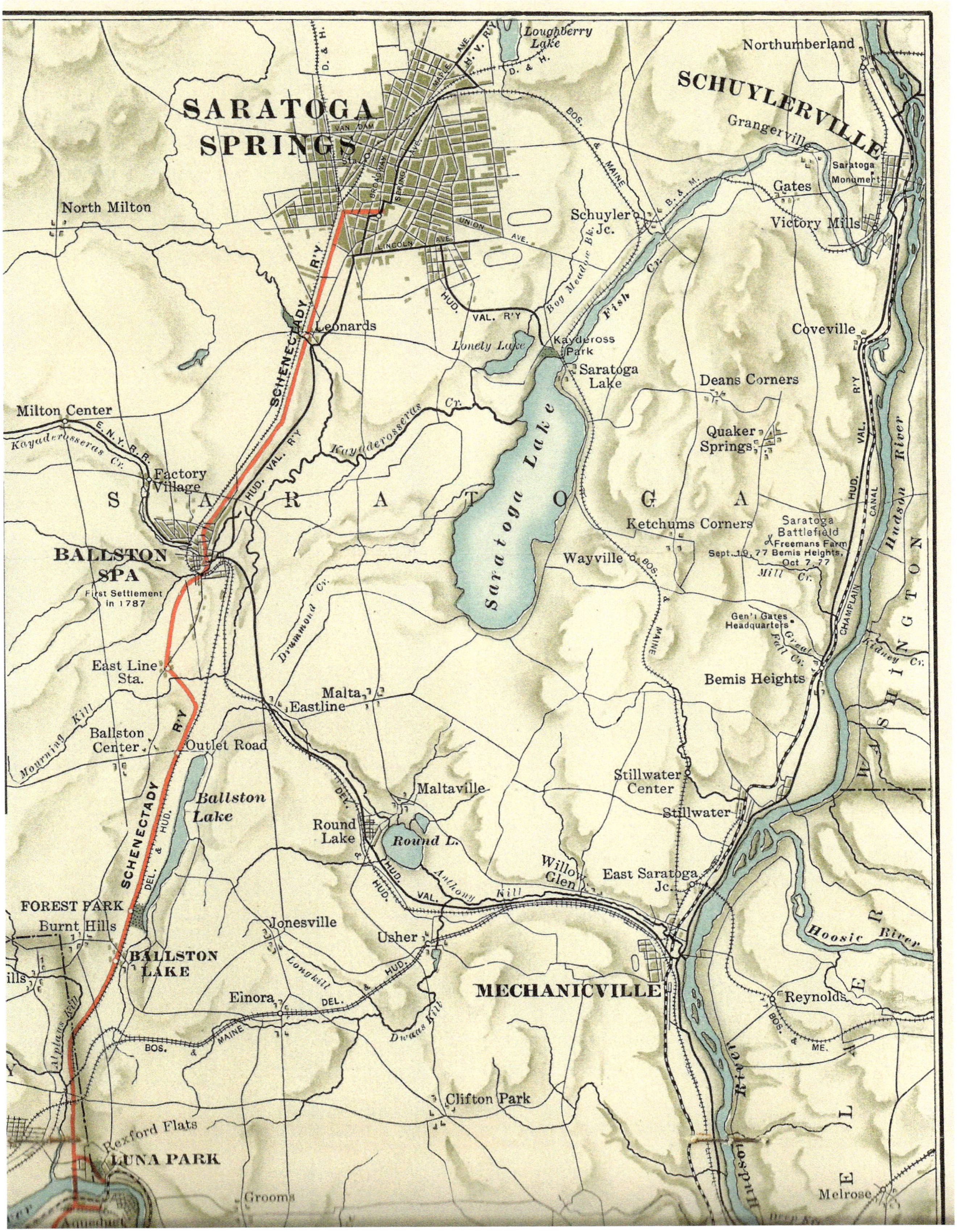

(Author's collection)

(Author's collection)

(Author's collection)

Appendix VI

Schenectady Railway Interurban Stops

The stops on the interurban lines from Schenectady are listed in the following tables and shown on the following maps. Schenectady Railway first assigned numbers to each of the trolley stops on the Albany and Troy interurban lines in 1903. Stop numbers and locations on these lines were subsequently adjusted as the city expanded outward. The source for the lists presented here is undated but appears to reflect the location of the stops for most of the interurban area. The practice of numbering stops was shared with another New York Central-owned interurban company, New York State Railways. These numbers were commonly used by the general public to identify locations.

The 0-mile point for the three Schenectady Railway tables is the Fuller Street barn. The 1913 Schenectady waiting room was not identified in the tables, but it was located at approximately mile 0.7.

The Fonda, Johnstown and Gloversville did not use numbers to identify stops on its lines. The location of the Schenectady stop in the table is the waiting room.

0	Schenectady	0.00	17	Karmers	8.07
1	Alvey Street	2.77	18	Browns	8.28
2	Commercial Hotel	3.03	19	Cramers	8.51
3	Hastings	3.17	20	Whites	8.83
4	Van Zandts	3.46	20½	Reeses	9.11
4½	Gebhard Street	3.65	21	Rapps	9.36
5	Chiswell Street	3.83	22	The Elms	9.65
5½	Steers	4.11	22½	Hennessys	9.92
6	Stanfords *	4.25	23	Scaces *	10.03
7	Fagans	4.63	24	Cemetery	10.32
8	Dennicks	5.01	25	Waldorfs	10.47
9	Uplands	5.29	26	Mountain View	10.65
10	Ostroms	5.52	27	Lockrows	10.86
11	Lishas Kill Church	5.73	28	Dotts	11.09
12	Lishas Kill Store	6.16	29	Roessleville	11.26
13	Vonies	6.36	30	McNutts	11.45
14	Van Hoesens *	6.70	31	Culvert (West)	11.71
14½	Olivers	7.12	32	Culvert (East)	11.90
15	Bruschabers	7.47	32½	Frosts *	12.06
16	Sub-Station	7.97	33	Albany City Line	12.31

34	Shaffers	12.42	37	West Albany	13.04
35	Vigars	12.78	38	Albany	15.55
36	Welchs	12.93			

* Limit of fare zones

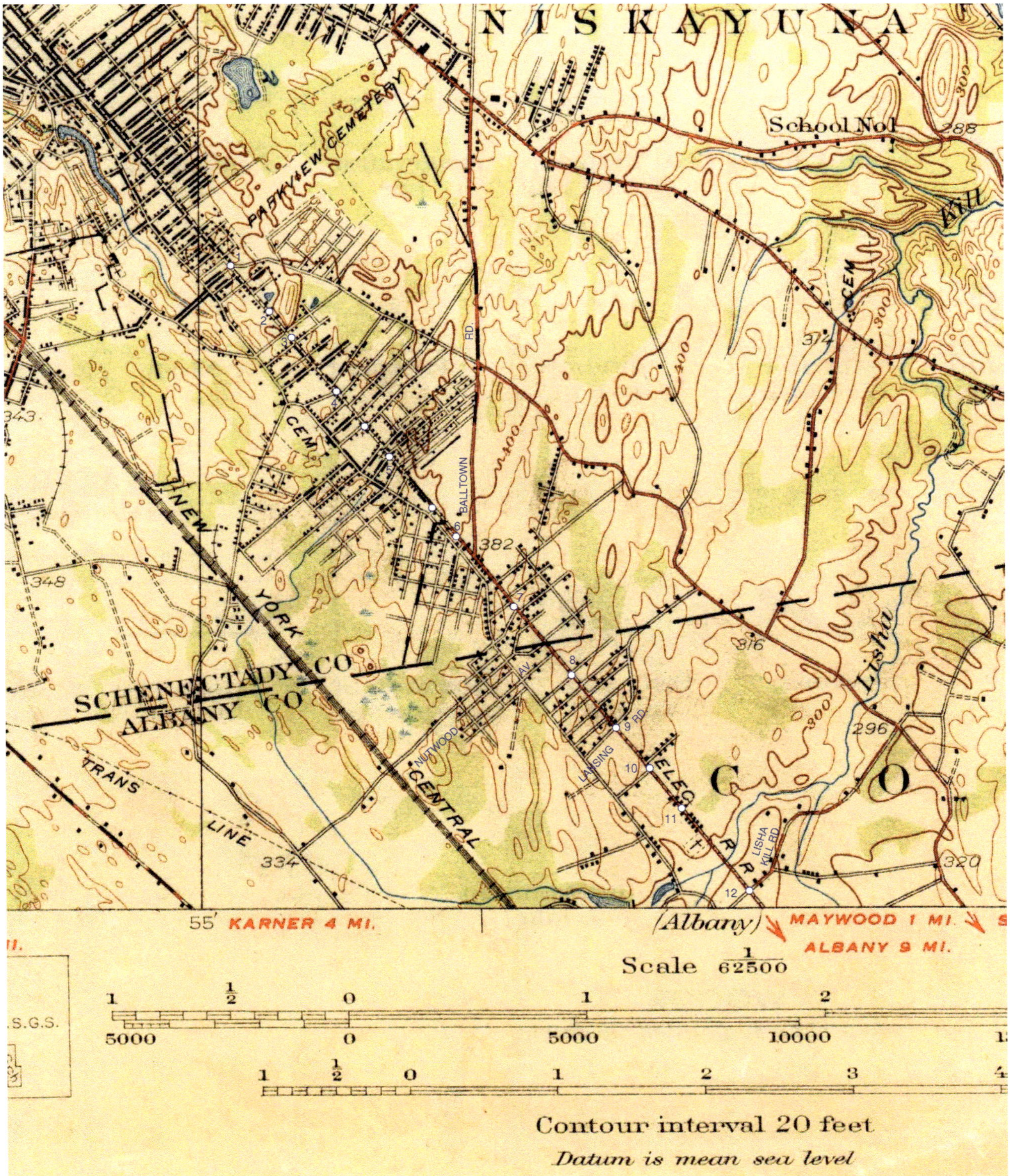

(U.S. Geological Survey with annotations added by author)

(U.S. Geological Survey with annotations added by author)

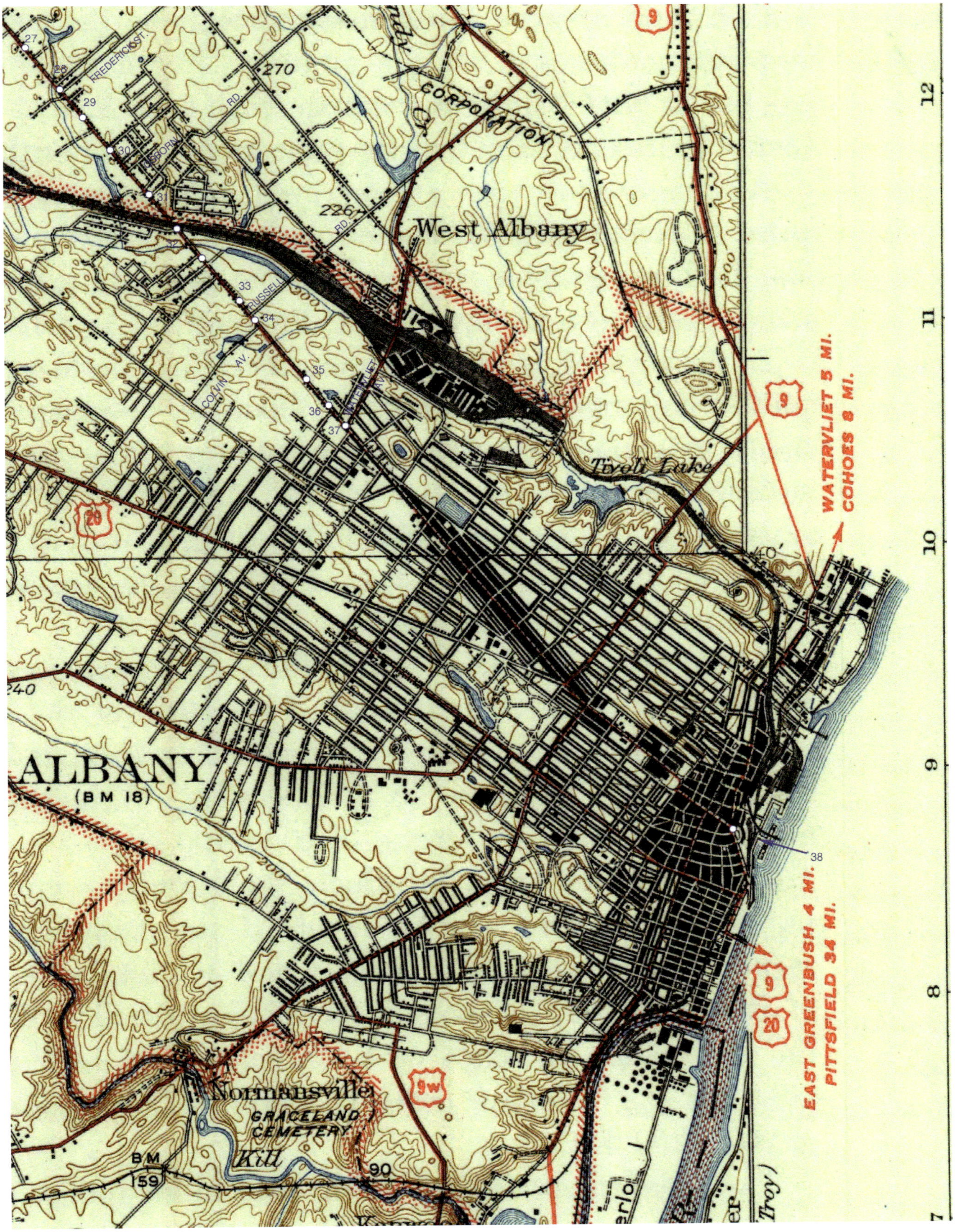

(U.S. Geological Survey with annotations added by author)

0	Schenectady	0.00	24	Orlops	8.25
1	Teagles	3.48	25	Shaker Road	8.47
2	Dye Works	3.62	26	Morrissville	8.71
3	Hammonds	3.73	27	Van Valkenburgs	8.81
4	Balltown Road	3.81	28	Hess's	8.88
5	Golf Club	3.87	29	Knadler's Hotel	9.03
6	Chatains	3.92	30	Albany Road	9.11
7	Huntings	4.04	30½	Best's	9.25
8	Rosendale Road	4.13	31	The Pines	9.38
9	St. David's Lane	4.22	31½	Knadlers	9.68
10	Taylors *	4.40	32	Ladues	10.27
11	Stones	4.68	33	Seven Oaks	10.62
12	Jones	4.77	33½	Wades	10.70
13	Mesicks C.	5.29	34	Maplewood	10.93
14	Pearse Road	5.66	34½	Gaffers	11.20
14½	Hawleys	5.93	35	Nine Elms	11.40
15	Steel Bridge	5.95	36	Lathams *	11.66
15½	Creigers	6.09	36½	McNabs	11.89
16	Mesicks	6.39	37	Kalflashs	12.23
16½	Mohawk Road	6.46	38	Idle Ways	12.55
17	Lishas Kill Road	6.59	39	Goodrichs	12.84
17½	Altrocks	6.75	39½	Youngs	12.92
18	Scarffs	6.94	40	Private Right of Way	13.04
19	Marks	7.07	41	Boulevards	13.26
19½	Drydens	7.21	42	Wiswalls *	14.12
20	Van Vrankens	7.32	43	12th Avenue and 16th Street, Watervliet	14.44
21	Reformed Church	7.43	44	12th Avenue and 19th Street, Watervliet	14.75
22	Riverview Road	7.49		(3rd Avenue and 25th Street, Watervliet)	15.59
23	Niskayuna *	7.83	45	Troy	16.86

* Limit of fare zones

(U.S. Geological Survey with annotations added by author)

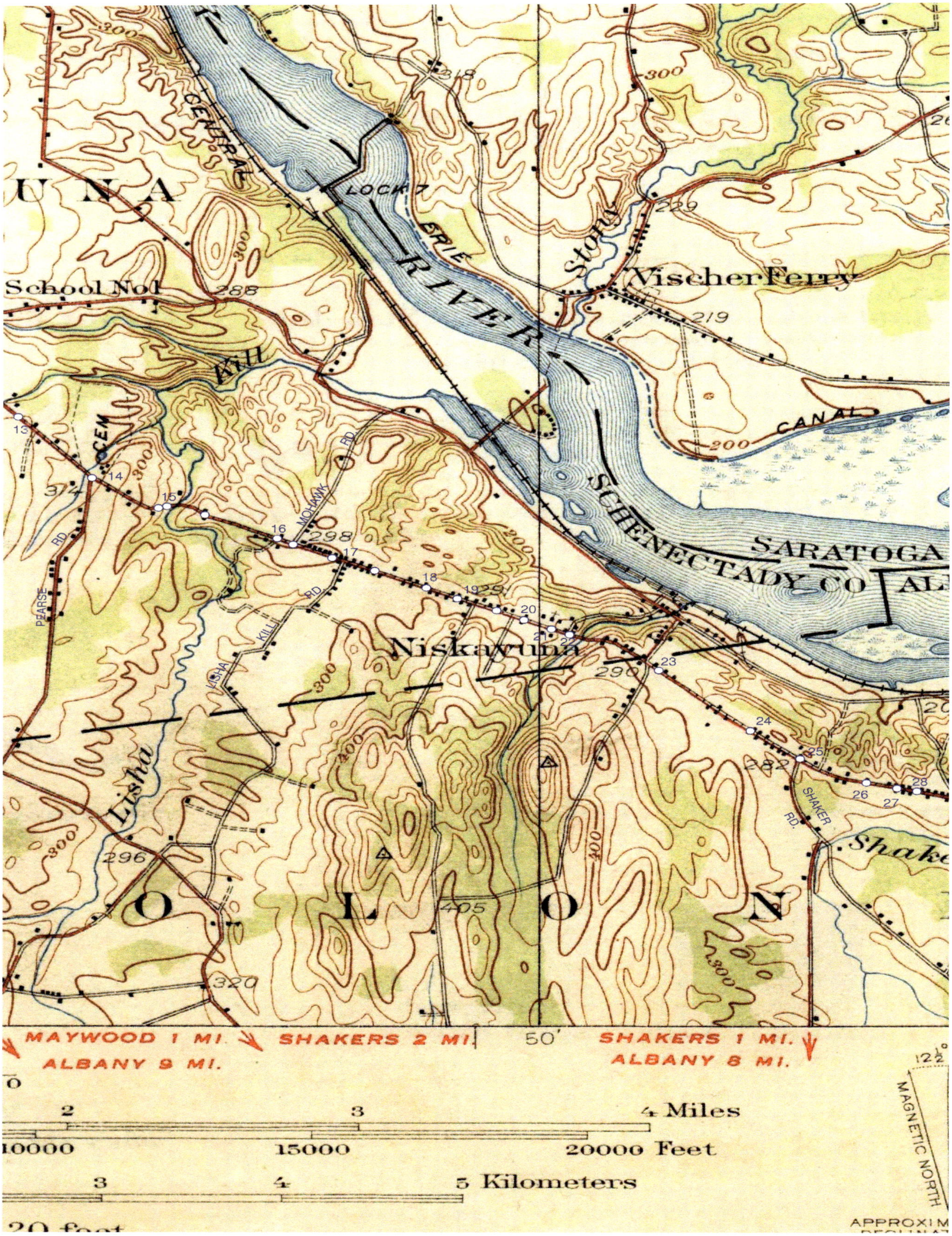

(U.S. Geological Survey with annotations added by author)

(U.S. Geological Survey with annotations added by author)

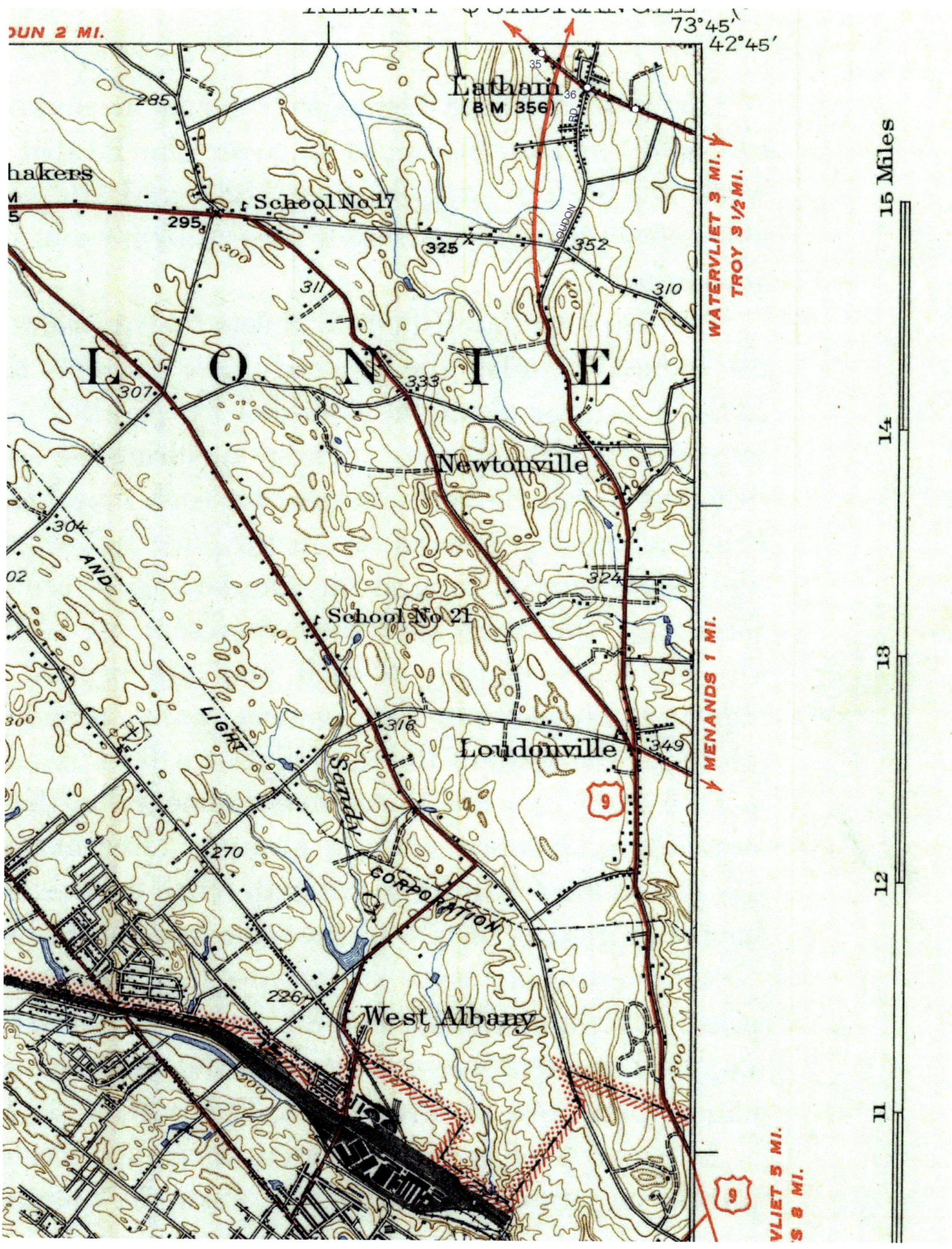

(U.S. Geological Survey with annotations added by author)

(U.S. Geological Survey with annotations added by author)

0	Schenectady	0.00	10	Buells	11.36	20	Hodges	18.54
1	Alplaus *	4.65	11	Lakeview	11.62	21	Harris	19.11
2	Madisons	5.45	12	Hazelwood	11.71	22	Leonards	19.43
3	Burnt Hills *	7.36	13	Outlet Road	12.17	23	Carlsbad	19.89
4	Ballston Lake	8.79	14	East Line *	13.65	24	Geyser	20.55
5	Forest Park	9.10	15	Main Road	13.91	25	Oil Tank	21.01
6	Oakwood	9.28	16	Garretts	15.16	26	Baker & Shevlins	21.45
7	Timesons *	9.98	17	Ballston Spa	16.10	27	Saratoga	22.39
8	Hawkwood	10.84	18	Ballston Junction *	16.84			
9	Nettletons	11.16	19	Grays	17.62			

* Limit of fare zones

(U.S. Geological Survey with annotations added by author)

(U.S. Geological Survey with annotations added by author)

(U.S. Geological Survey with annotations added by author)

Stop	Mile
Gloversville Electric Sta.	0.00
Johnstown	4.05
Sulphur Spring Junction	5.74
Albany Bush	7.73
Browers'	9.05
Tribes Hill upper crossing	11.07
Tribes Hill lower crossing	11.53
Antlers	12.17
Fort Johnson	13.53
W. Main Street Junction	14.47
Henrietta Street	15.19
Market Street	16.37
Amsterdam	16.58
Lark Street	17.15
Ross' Crossover	17.55
DeGraff's	18.32
Truax	19.03
Cranesville	19.84
Hoffmans	23.18
Johnsons	24.54
Reynolds	25.88
Urban	26.57
Rectors	27.23
Wyatts	28.01
Hardins	29.53
Tower Nine	30.52
B&M Bridge	31.02
Scotia Junction	32.03
Schenectady	33.01

(*U.S. Geological Survey with annotations added by author*)

(U.S. Geological Survey with annotations added by author)

(U.S. Geological Survey with annotations added by author)

(U.S. Geological Survey with annotations added by author)

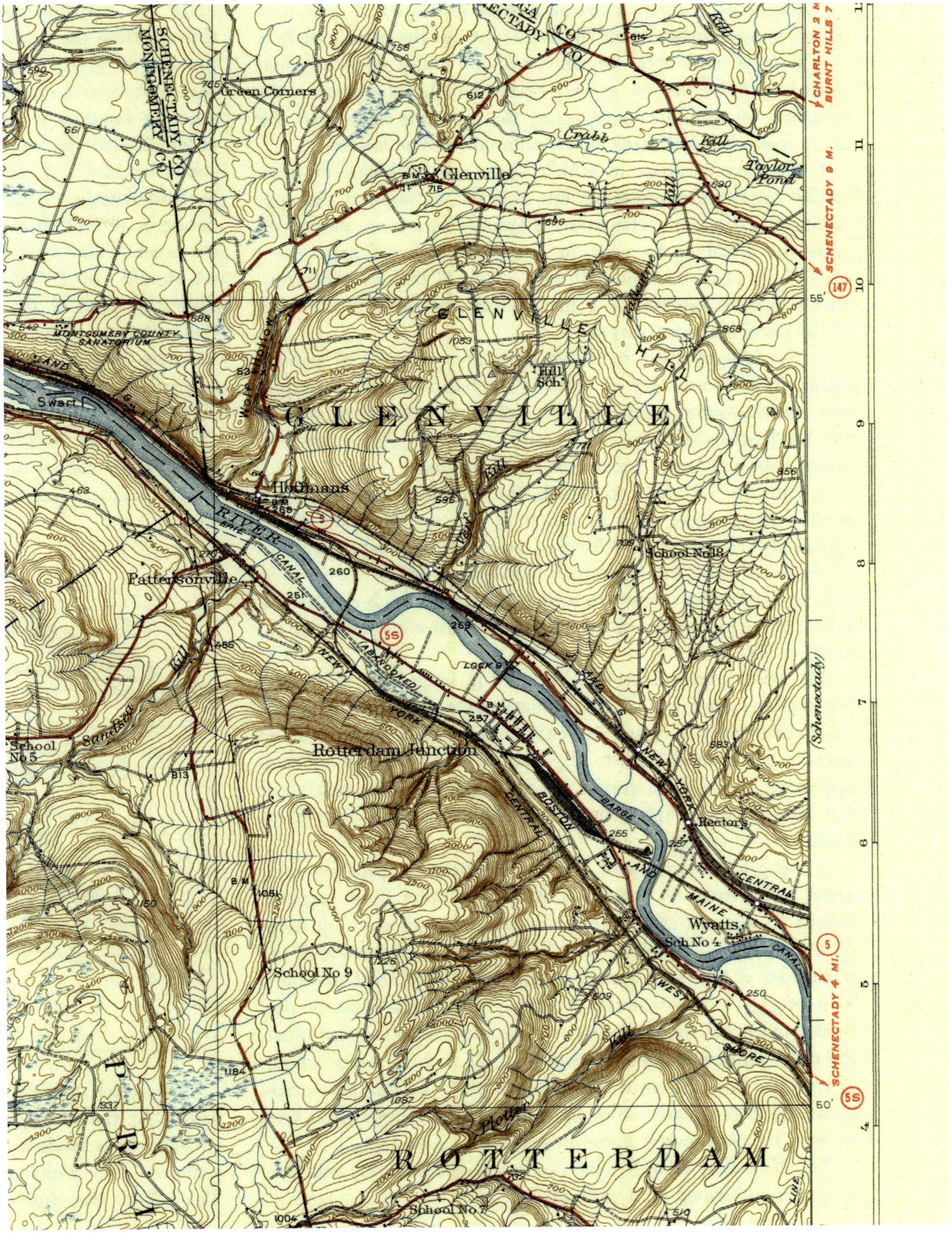

(U.S. Geological Survey with annotations added by author)

(U.S. Geological Survey with annotations added by author)

Appendix VII

Electric Power

A single streetcar can consume a considerable amount of power. Even in the early years of street railways, one car could demand 37,300 W (50 hp) of power, and this figure increased substantially as newer, larger, and faster cars were built. The electric power system had to keep pace with all of this growing demand. Street railways were thus one of the first large-scale applications of electricity, and their development was intertwined with the development of the electric power grid.

G.1 Schenectady Railway

The power system for Schenectady Railway was generally quite typical for a street railway, but it had some unusual characteristics, as it was fed by one of the earliest electric power grids in America. Initially, power was produced at a powerhouse on Dock Street with dynamos (direct current (DC) generators). The power was produced at a potential of 600 V and fed directly into copper contact wires over each track. Feeder wires were usually strung in parallel and connected to the contact wires at regular intervals (e.g., every 500 feet) to provide additional current-carrying capability. Each streetcar had a pole (or two) on the roof with a wheel on the end; the wheel contacted the overhead wire to provide electricity to the motors.[1] The rails were used for the return current path. Although the potential of the contact wires was nominally 600 V, the actual voltage varied widely with the changes in electrical load as the vehicles accelerated and decelerated.

Naturally, the large expansion of in-city and interurban routes between 1899 and 1904 required a commensurate increase in power. Most of this power was obtained from the Hudson River Water Power Company and its hydro plants. High voltage alternating current (AC) transmission was constructed to bring in the power from the relatively distant power plants. In order for the DC motors to use this power, rotary converters were installed at key locations to feed the AC power into the DC trolley system.[2]

Two 10-kV AC lines brought power from the new Mechanicville hydro-station on the Hudson River. This station produced AC electricity at a frequency of 40 Hz and was capable of generating 5.2 MW of electrical power.[3] The transmission fed three substations with AC transformers and rotary converters to transform the 10-kV AC power into 600-V DC for the trolley wires. One substation was located in a new building at Dock Street, which replaced the original powerhouse, while the other two were located at Lathams and Karners to power the new interurban lines to Troy and Albany respectively. Supplementary power was obtained from generation at the G.E. Works.

Another hydro plant with 24 MW of generating capacity was constructed at Spier Falls and began producing power in 1903. AC transmission lines of 30-kV potential were constructed to bring the power to the cities of the Capital District. Like Mechanicville, Spier Falls generated power at 40 Hz. A fourth substation was constructed at Ballston to power the Ballston extension by tapping one of the 30-kV transmission lines.

A view of the Albany interurban trackage, westward from Stop 20, showing the overhead electrical structure. The contact wire over each track is supported by span wires between the poles at regular intervals. The contact wires are fastened to the span wires through insulators. Two DC feeder wires are supported by the lower cross arms on the poles on the far side of the tracks. A connection from one of the DC feeders to the contact wires is visible at the second pole from the right. (*From the collection of the Efner History Center at City Hall, Schenectady*)

Inside the substation at Karner's on the Albany line. Rotary converters may be seen on the left. (*From the collection of the Efner History Center at City Hall, Schenectady*)

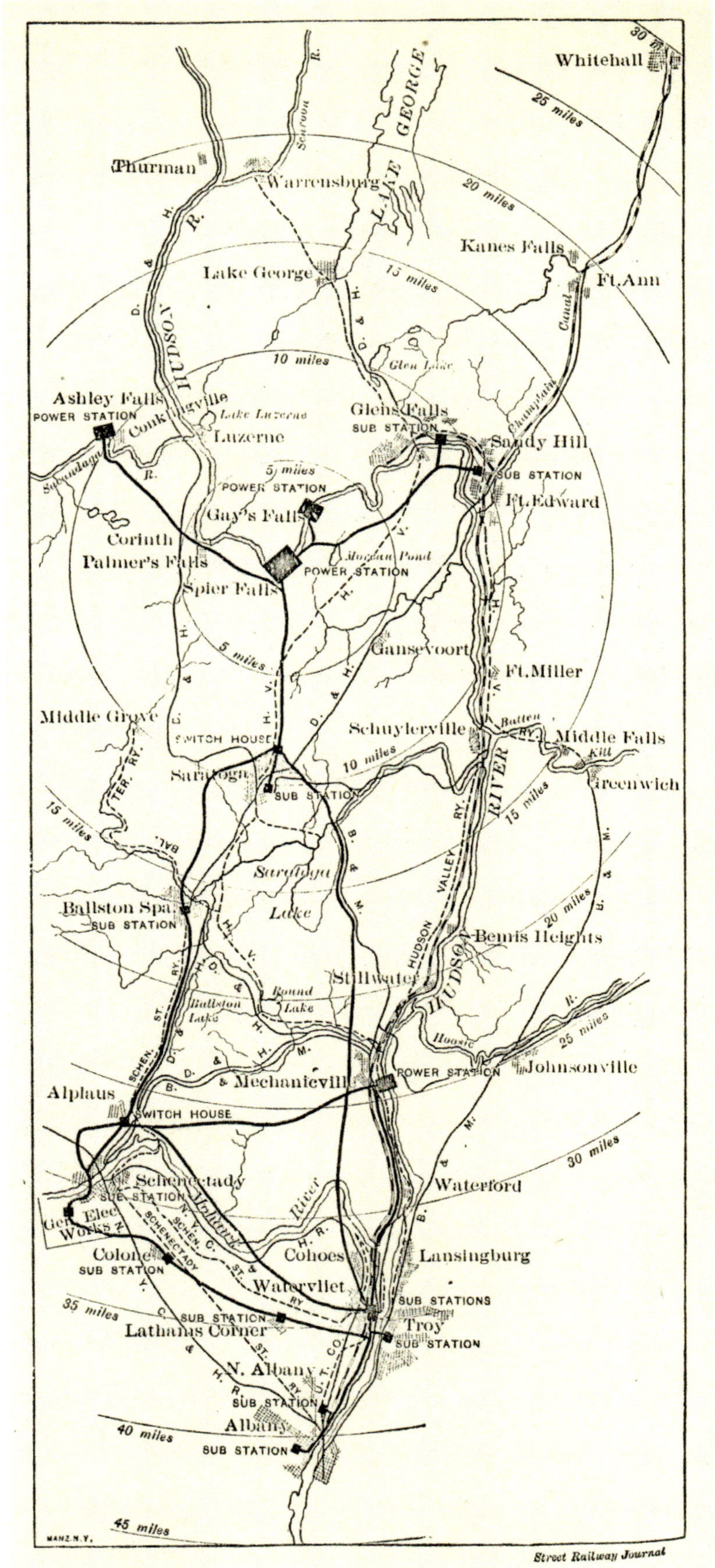

The transmission system of the Hudson River Water Power Company, 1903. (*From the collection of the Schenectady County Historical Society*)

When the Ballston line opened in 1904, it had an unusual dual-power overhead catenary system. A 600-V DC trolley wire was carried over the center of the trackway, just as with conventional overhead catenary; however, an additional 2,200-V AC contact wire was provided on the side. General Electric used this power for conducting experiments with a "compensated motor," which, it was hoped, would be the next breakthrough in electric transportation. G.E. had an experimental vehicle that operated on the track to test the new motors. The vehicle was dual-powered; with the push of a button, it could switch between 2,200-V AC and 600-V DC, the latter being necessary for in-city operation. Ultimately, the experiments were deemed unsuccessful, and the vehicle was withdrawn after about a year.

G.2 Fonda, Johnstown and Gloversville

FJ&G constructed a power generation and transmission system in conjunction with its interurban line between Johnstown and Schenectady. A 3-MW coal-fired power plant was built at Tribes Hill. This plant fed a 13.2-kV, 25-Hz AC transmission line which ran atop the power poles that supported the catenary for the interurban line. Three substations with rotary converters—located at Johnstown, Amsterdam, and Glenville—fed the DC catenary, which consisted of two 0000-gauge copper contact wires (one for each track, each with resistance 0.26 Ω/mile), one 300-kcmil feeder wire (resistance: 0.18 Ω/mile), and one 500-kcmil feeder wire (resistance: 0.11 Ω/mile).[4] The two feeders and two trolley wires were tied together every 500 feet.

(Schenectady Union-Star, Schenectady County Public Library)

Endnotes

Chapter 2

1 It is difficult to imagine a company undertaking construction on such a basis today.

2 In 1892, Edison General Electric and Thomson Electric would merge to form General Electric.

Chapter 3

1 The Schenectady City Council had previously approved a franchise for this branch, but the street railway company was unable to start construction, and the street railway withdrew its request for an extension of time.

Chapter 4

1 By this time, double-track was generally permitted under the city's franchises.

2 Annexation took place by an act of the state legislature (chapter 204, laws of 1902); no significant opposition to the annexation was expressed from representatives of the affected neighborhoods at city council meetings on the matter.

Chapter 5

1 The mileage figure quoted here is for the stretch of railway constructed east of the intersection with Elbert Street, which became the location of the city boundary after the 1902 annexation.

2 From the October 1907 Schenectady Railway timetable.

3 From a 1910 FJ&G timetable.

4 Hudson Valley Railway was an amalgamation of several local street railways into an interurban system that connected Troy, Mechanicville, Saratoga Springs, Schuylerville, Glens Falls, and Warrensburg.

5 This section of steam railroad track was built in 1832 by the Saratoga and Schenectady Railroad.

6 From the October 1907 Schenectady Railway timetable.

7 There were actually two locations named Ballston Junction. H.V.R.C. reached Ballston Spa with a 0.9-mile spur off of its Mechanicville–Saratoga Springs line; the point where this spur joined the main line was named Ballston Junction. The name "Ballston Junction" was also later applied to the location where the Schenectady Railway trackage met the D&H steam tracks north of Ballston Spa.

8 At the time, Hudson Valley Railway had no depot for passengers in Saratoga Springs; thus, the "terminal" was essentially just the end of the track.

9 From the October 1907 Schenectady Railway timetable.

Chapter 7

1 The crossing was still in use in the middle of 1906 but had been removed by the middle of 1908.

2 This arrangement resulted in the odd situation of Schenectady Railway having to pay to use its own tracks between Lincoln Center and Ballston Junction.

Chapter 8

1 The FJ&G line to Gloversville constitutes 33.2 miles of this total: 33.0 miles from Schenectady to downtown Gloversville plus an additional 0.2 miles to the Gloversville steam railroad station. The 71.5-mile total for Schenectady Railway routes is the sum of the "first track" mileage figure of 60.0 from the 1918 P.S.C. report plus the additional 3.2 miles to Albany, 2.8 miles to Troy, and 6.5 miles to Saratoga Springs over the rails of other companies and minus the 1.05 miles of Schenectady Railway trackage that were counted as part of the FJ&G Gloversville route.

Chapter 10

1 The author has personal experience with these cars, having ridden them on the ex-P&W Norristown High-Speed Line, now Southeastern Pennsylvania Transportation Authority (S.E.P.T.A.) Route 100.

2 For the same reason, the entire street railway industry would soon assemble a committee to design a standardized modern vehicle. The resulting vehicles were known as Presidents' Conference Committee (PCC) cars. A large quantity was collectively produced by many streetcar builders and used in many cities, with some success in retaining riders. PCC cars were not used in Schenectady, however. Brill did not participate and instead produced its own streamlined designs; the Bullets were one of those designs.

Appendix VII

1 The wheel "trolled" the contact wire as the streetcar moved along; hence, the term "trolley" actually refers to this wheel. Over time, however, the term "trolley" was commonly applied to the entire vehicle.

2 A rotary converter is essentially an AC motor and a DC generator in a single rotating unit.

3 This power station, still operating as of this writing, has a unique claim to having operated in three centuries: the nineteenth, twentieth, and twenty-first.

4 One circular mil (cmil) is the area of a circle with a diameter of one mil (0.001 inch). The unit usually refers to the cross section of a wire. 1 kcmil = 1,000 cmil.

Bibliography

The American Architect, Vol. CVII, No. 2061, June 23, 1915

Bankat, J., "New Cars for Schenectady Railway," *Street Railway Review*, Vol. XIV, No. 6, June 20, 2004, pp. 421-424

Brill, D., *History of the J. G. Brill Company* (Bloomington, IN: Indiana University Press, 2001)

Buell, B., "Plan Bee Got an 'A,'" *Schenectady Gazette*, March 25, 2014, pp. C4-C5

Burch, E., *Electric Traction for Railway Trains* (NY: McGraw-Hill, 1911), pp. 136-141

Cox, H., "Schenectady Railway Co. Roster of Cars," undated. Available at http://donsdepot.donrossgroup.net/dr0105/schyroster.jpg, accessed June 15, 2018

Daily Union, "A Silver Spike. The Street Railway to be Formally Completed To-Morrow.," July 14, 1887

Daily Union, "The Last Spike Driven," July 16, 1887, p. 3

Daily Union, "East Avenue Place," July 1, 1891, p. 4

Daily Union, "With a Buzz and Whir," July 3, 1891, p. 3

Daily Union, "Local Notes," July 25, 1891, p. 3

Daily Union, "Local Notes," July 27, 1891, p. 4

Daily Union, "The Common Council," August 12, 1891, p. 2

Daily Union, "Local Notes," September 11, 1891, p. 3

Daily Union, "The Bellevue Extension," October 17, 1891, p. 3

Daily Union, "Local Notes," October 19, 1891, p. 3

Daily Union, "Local Notes," May 30, 1892, p. 3

Daily Union, "Local Notes," June 12, 1893, p. 3

Daily Union, "Schenectady Street Railway Company," January 4, 1895

Daily Union, "Schenectady St Railway; Certificate of Re-organization Filed With the Secretary of State," February 12, 1895, p. 5

Daily Union, "Local Notes," April 29, 1895

Daily Union, "Bought It All," August 6, 1898, p. 1

Daily Union, "Extension In Operation," September 30, 1899, p. 1

Daily Union, "All the Way Now," October 20, 1899

Daily Union, "By Trolley to Albany," September 10, 1901

Daily Union, "Schenectady Railway Co.," October 1, 1901, p. 7

Daily Union, "The Greater Schenectady," March 22, 1902, p. 7

Daily Union, "The Schenectady Railway Company," August 22, 1902

Daily Union, "Schenectady Railway Co.," August 25, 1902

Daily Union, "Six New Cars Here," March 20, 1903

Daily Union, "Cars to be Renumbered," March 20, 1903
Daily Union, "Trolley to Ninth Ward," May 29, 1903
Daily Union, "Railway Numbering All Stops," September 1, 1903
Daily Union, "Bridge Cotton Factory Hollow [editorial]," November 12, 1903
Daily Union, "Ballston Line Open," June 30, 1904, p. 2
Daily Union, "Open to the End," July 2, 1904, p. 2
Daily Union, "The Winter Time Card," September 23, 1904
Daily Union, "Belt Lines on Monday," December 2, 1905, p. 1
Daily Union, "City and Railway Are At Odds," September 11, 1907, p. 1
Daily Union, "P. S. Board Sustains Railway," April 19, 1911, p. 1
Daily Union, "Franchises Granted," July 18, 1911, p. 1
Decker, R., *The Fonda, Johnstown, & Gloversville Railroad* (Charleston, SC: Arcadia Publishing, 1998)
DiCarlo, G., *Trolleys of the Capital District* (Charleston, SC: Arcadia Publishing, 2009)
Electric Railway Journal, "Schenectady Fare Case Decided in Favor of Company," Vol. XLIII, No. 22, May 30, 1914, pp. 1232-1233
Evening Star, "The Street Railway. Schenectady's Street Railway to be Pushed Forward to Completion at Once—Locating the Barn and Stables," October 28, 1886, p. 3
Evening Star, "The Street Railway. The Completion of the Road to be Celebrated To-Morrow Evening by the Driving of a Silver Spike, and Oratorical Exercises.," July 14, 1887, p. 3
Evening Star, "Driving the Silver Spike," July 16, 1887, p. 3
Evening Star, "Auction Sale of Horses!," July 16, 1891, p. 1
Evening Star, "The Street Railway Sold," January 3, 1895
Evening Star, "The Street Railway. A New Company to be Organized by the Purchasers.," January 4, 1895
Evening Star, "Passing of Scotia Bus.," April 16, 1902
Evening Star, "Belt Line Service," September 17, 1902, p. 5
Evening Star, "End Made to Trolley Fight," April 21, 1903, p. 1
Evening Star, "Expanding With the Town," October 9, 1903
Farrell, M., *The History of Baltimore's Streetcars* (Sykesville, MD: Greenberg Publishing Co., 1992)
Gagne, J., "Present Rail Operations of Schenectady Rwy. Co.," diagram, November 1942
Google, Google Maps, http://www.google.com/maps, 2017-18. Retrieved December 2017-May 2018
Gordon, W., and Mowers, R., *Trolley's [sic] Down the Mohawk Valley* (Rochester, NY: William Reed Gordon, c. 1968)
Hart, L., *Schenectady: A Pictorial History, Second Edition* (Scotia, NY: Old Dorp Books, 1990)
Hart, L., "Electricity Doomed Brief Day of Horsecar," *Schenectady Union-Star*, July 26, 1960, p. 2
Hart, L., "Trolley Tracks Blossomed Almost Overnight," *Schenectady Union-Star*, August 2, 1960
Hart, L., "Trolley System Caused Evolution of Cities," *Schenectady Union-Star*, August 9, 1960, p. 6
Hart, L., "Miss Levi Wins Battle Against Trolley Firm," *Schenectady Union-Star*, August 30, 1960
Hart, L., "Trolley Bridge Linked to City's Progress," *Schenectady Union-Star*, September 6, 1960
Hart, L., "The Wildest Streetcar Ride in City's History," *Schenectady Union-Star*, September 13, 1960
Hart, L., "City Progress Parallels Gas Industry Growth," *Schenectady Union-Star*, September 20, 1960
Hart, L., "Lawsuits Plagued Trolley Expansion Efforts," *Schenectady Union-Star*, September 27, 1960
Hart, L., "Carbarns Once Hard-Pressed to Meet Needs," *Schenectady Union-Star*, October 11, 1960
Hart, L., "Trolleys Found Ways to Meet Emergencies," *Schenectady Union-Star*, October 25, 1960
Hart, L., "Ballston Spa Becomes Site of 'Trolley War'," *Schenectady Union-Star*, November 1, 1960
Hart, L., "Parks Swelled Business for Trolley Lines," *Schenectady Union-Star*, November 15, 1960
Hart, L., "Electric Street Lighting Came to Scotia in 1903," *Schenectady Union-Star*, November 22, 1960
Hart, L., "90-Year Evolution of a Railroad Enterprise," *Schenectady Union-Star*, November 29, 1960
Hart, L., "Told and Retold Stories From the Trolley Days," *Schenectady Union-Star*, December 6, 1960, p. 6
Hart, L., "Brief, Illustrious Life of Local Trolley Waiting Room," *Schenectady Union-Star*, December 13, 1960

Hart, L., "Street Rioting Flamed in 1923 Trolley Strike," *Schenectady Union-Star*, December 20, 1960

Hart, L., "Automobile Age Tolled Dirge for Streetcars; Motorized Buses Gradually Took Over Here," *Schenectady Union-Star*, December 27, 1960

Hart, L., "Era of trolleys ended in Scotia when buses took over in 1931," *Schenectady Gazette*, November 2, 1997, p. B12

JIMAPCO, *Greater Capital Region 11 County Atlas*, 5th Ed.,(Round Lake, NY: JIMAPCO, 2007)

Journal of the Common Council of the City of Schenectady, 1885-86

Journal of the Common Council of the City of Schenectady, 1886-87

Journal of the Common Council of the City of Schenectady, 1890-91

Journal of the Common Council of the City of Schenectady, 1891-92

Journal of the Common Council of the City of Schenectady, 1892-93

Journal of the Common Council of the City of Schenectady, 1893-94

Journal of the Common Council of the City of Schenectady, 1894-95

Journal of the Common Council of the City of Schenectady, 1896-98

Journal of the Common Council of the City of Schenectady, 1898

Journal of the Common Council of the City of Schenectady, 1899

Journal of the Common Council of the City of Schenectady, 1900

Journal of the Common Council of the City of Schenectady, 1901

Journal of the Common Council of the City of Schenectady, 1902

Journal of the Common Council of the City of Schenectady, 1903

Levine, H., "City Railway Started With 'Giddyap' in '86," *Schenectady Union-Star*, June 26, 1948, p. 25A

Maston, B., *An Enclave of Elegance* (Schenectady, NY: G.E.P.R.A. Publications, 1983)

Miller, D., *Atlas of the City of Schenectady, New York* (Philadelphia, PA: D. L. Miller & A. H. Mueller, 1905)

Mowers, R., "Electric Cars in the Electric City," *Electric Traction Quarterly*, Vol. 3, No. 1, 2, Fall/Winter 1964

Nestle, D., and Gordon, W., *Steam and Trolley Days on the Fonda, Johnstown and Gloversville Railroad* (Self-published, 1958)

Nestle, D., *A History of the Hudson Valley Railway* (Self-published, 1967)

Proceedings of the Common Council of the City of Schenectady, 1904

Proceedings of the Common Council of the City of Schenectady, 1905

Proceedings of the Common Council of the City of Schenectady, 1906

Proceedings of the Common Council of the City of Schenectady, 1907

Proceedings of the Common Council of the City of Schenectady, 1908

Proceedings of the Common Council of the City of Schenectady, 1909

Proceedings of the Common Council of the City of Schenectady, 1910

Proceedings of the Common Council of the City of Schenectady, 1911

Proceedings of the Common Council of the City of Schenectady, 1912

Proceedings of the Common Council of the City of Schenectady, 1914

Proceedings of the Common Council of the City of Schenectady, 1915

Proceedings of the Common Council of the City of Schenectady, 1918

Proceedings of the Common Council of the City of Schenectady, 1919

Proceedings of the Common Council of the City of Schenectady, 1920

Proceedings of the Common Council of the City of Schenectady, 1922

Proceedings of the Common Council together with Message of the Mayor and Reports of City Officers of the City of Schenectady for the Year 1909, and General Ordinances As Revised to March 28, 1910

Proceedings of the Common Council together with Message of the Mayor and Reports of City Officers of the City of Schenectady for the Year 1912

Poulin, Francis A., Francis Poulin Scrapbook Collection, Volume 8, Grems-Doolittle Library and Archives, Schenectady, NY

The Railway News, "Electric Traction in America," Vol. LXXXIII, March 4, 1905, pp. 373-375

Reports of Decisions of the Public Service Commission Second District of the State of New York, Vol. II, 1911

Rittner, D., *Schenectady: Frontier Village to Colonial City* (Charleston, SC: The History Press, 2011)
Rockwell, H., *Street Railway Review*, "The Electric Division of the Fonda, Johnstown & Gloversville Railroad," Vol. XIII, No. 8, August 20, 1903, pp. 485-497
Schenectady County Historical Society, Schenectady Railway file, Grems-Doolittle Library and Archives, Schenectady, NY
Schenectady Gazette, "First Car Makes Trip to Scotia," April 16, 1902
Schenectady Gazette, "Scotia Cars are Running No [sic] Schedule," April 17, 1902
Schenectady Gazette, "Trolley Line to Aqueduct Will Be Opened Saturday," August 18, 1902
Schenectady Gazette, "Cars to Run on New Bellevue Line," November 12, 1902
Schenectady Gazette, "'Carnival of Months,'" November 13, 1902
Schenectady Gazette, "Watervliet Cars Don't Run All the Way," November 17, 1902, p. 2
Schenectady Gazette, "Watervliet Trouble Over," November 18, 1902, p. 1
Schenectady Gazette, "Schenectady Railway Co. Time Table," November 18, 1902
Schenectady Gazette, "Upper Broadway Trolley Tracks Used Yesterday," December 8, 1902, p. 5
Schenectady Gazette, "Cars are Running to Troy," March 3, 1903
Schenectady Gazette, "Trolley Cars To Have New Numbers," March 21, 1903
Schenectady Gazette, "Trolley War Ends," April 22, 1902
Schenectady Gazette, "Trolley Line for Ninth Ward Soon," May 29, 1903, p. 8
Schenectady Gazette, "State Street Lighting Will Be Much Improved," April 13, 1904
Schenectady Gazette, "Trolley Direct to Saratoga," August 1, 1904, p. 4
Schenectady Gazette, "Rushing New Line," March 30, 1905, p. 5
Schenectady Gazette, "Line Nearly Done," March 31, 1905
Schenectady Gazette, "New Trolley Line is Open," April 1, 1905
Schenectady Gazette, "Aldermen Inspect 'Subway' Details," March 30, 1905
Schenectady Gazette, "'Subway' Put on the Table by Aldermen," April 14, 1905, p. 1
Schenectady Gazette, "Schenectady Railway Gets Right of Way to Saratoga," April 5, 1906
Schenectady Gazette, "Public Utilities Bill is Now Law," June 7, 1907
Schenectady Gazette, "Scotia Compromise Urged," March 5, 1908
Schenectady Gazette, "Waiting Room to be Opened Today," October 21, 1913
Schenectady Gazette, "Waiting Room is Opened to Public," October 22, 1913, p. 1
Schenectady Gazette, "The New Railway Waiting Room [editorial]," October 22, 1913, p. 6
Schenectady Gazette, "Fare Increase Granted Local Railway Company," July 28, 1920
Schenectady Gazette, "Changes in Routes of 5 Trolley Line to Be Effective Tomorrow," February 4, 1930, p. 2
Schenectady Gazette, "Extension of Bus System Is Proposed," May 19, 1933
Schenectady Railway Company, "Trolley Trips, Hudson-Mohawk Valleys" brochure, undated (c. 1907)
Schenectady Transportation Guide, 1943
Schenectady Union-Star, "Schenectady a Trolley Centre for Half a Million People," October 19, 1913
Schenectady Union-Star, "New Schenectady Railway Waiting Room Opens at Noon Tomorrow," October 20, 1913
Schenectady Union-Star, "Crowds Visit Waiting Room," October 22, 1913
Schenectady Union-Star, "Seven-Cent Fare to Go in Effect Here in Few Days," July 28, 1920, p. 1
Schenectady Union-Star, "Increased Fares Effective Aug. 1," July 30, 1920, p. 1
Schenectady Union-Star, "Traction Bill Signed," March 31, 1921, p. 4
Shaughnessy, J., *Delaware & Hudson* (Syracuse, NY: Syracuse University Press, 1997)
Starr, T., *Early Railroads of New York's Capital District* (Rock City Falls, NY: Timothy Starr, 2011)
State of New York, *Twenty-Fourth Annual Report of the Board of Railroad Commissioners of the State of New York, 1906, Volume I, 1907*
State of New York, *Second Annual Report of the Public Service Commission Second District, for the Year Ended December 31, 1908, Volume I, 1909*

State of New York, *Fourth Annual Report of the Public Service Commission Second District, for the Year Ended December 31, 1910, Volume I, 1911*

State of New York, *Fifth Annual Report of the Public Service Commission Second District, for the Year Ended December 31, 1911, Volume I, 1912*

State of New York, *Sixth Annual Report of the Public Service Commission Second District, for the Year Ended December 31, 1912, Volume I, 1913*

State of New York, *Eighth Annual Report of the Public Service Commission Second District, for the Year Ended December 31, 1914, Volume I, 1915*

State of New York, *Ninth Annual Report of the Public Service Commission Second District, for the Year Ended December 31, 1915, Volume I, 1916*

State of New York, Laws of 1914, Chapter 58

State of New York, Laws of 1921, Chapter 134

State of New York, Laws of 1923, Chapter 336

Street Railway Journal, "Schenectady—Albany Trolley Line," Vol. XVIII, No. 13, September 28, 1901, pp. 357-358

Street Railway Journal, "Electric Railway Attractions at Saratoga and Vicinity," Vol. XXII, No. 9, August 29, 1903, pp. 288-328

Street Railway Journal, "Opening of the Saratoga-Schenectady Through Electric Line," Vol. XXX, No. 2, July 13, 1907, p. 69

Street Railway Review, "System of the Schenectady Railway Co.," Vol. XIII, No. 8, August 20, 1903, pp. 497-500

Sykes, F. G., *Street Railway Review*, "Power Supply and Distribution for the Schenectady Ry.," Vol. XIII, No. 8, August 20, 1903, pp. 500-502

Toman, J. and Hays, B., *Horse Trails to Regional Rails* (Kent, OH: Kent State University Press, 1996)

U.S. Geological Survey, Schenectady Sheet, New York, Edition of Dec. 1893

U.S. Geological Survey, Schenectady Sheet, New York, Edition of Mar. 1898

About the Author

Eric H. Allen, Ph.D., P.E. holds a doctor of philosophy degree in electrical engineering from the Massachusetts Institute of Technology and is currently employed as director of engineering at New England Transmission Software Solutions (N.E.T.S.S.), Inc. with over twenty years of experience in transmission planning and event analysis in the electric utility industry.

Although the author's primary employment is in the transportation of electrons, he is also a lifetime enthusiast of most forms of transportation, including in particular electric rail transit. He is a longtime member (twenty years) of several associations devoted to preserving and promoting the history of electric rail transit, including the Boston Street Railway Association (B.S.R.A.), the New York Transit Museum, and the Electric Railroaders' Association (E.R.A.). He has been a passenger on more than thirty American transit systems as well as several systems in Europe and Japan. He is also a member of the Schenectady County Historical Society.

Aside from the limitations imposed by private landowner rights, eighty years of vegetation growth, and a few alterations to the landscape, the author has personally traced, by car or on foot, almost every one of the 104.7 miles of ground once occupied by the tracks that carried trolleys in and out of Schenectady.